A Year C Reso

Contemporary Reflections

for praying and preaching

SHEILA WALKER

First published in 2006 by

KEVIN MAYHEW LTD
Buxhall, Stowmarket, Suffolk, IP14 3BW
info@kevinmayhewltd.com
www.kevinmayhew.com

9 8 7 6 5 4 3 2 1 0

ISBN 184417 661 4
Catalogue No. 1500927

Cover design by Sara-Jane Came
Edited by Sophia Sorrell
Typesetting by Richard Weaver

Printed and bound in Great Britain

Contents

EASTER

ORDINARY TIME

Foreword

Reflections are a bit risky: they're not carefully reasoned explanations of a passage, coming at it directly and tackling it in a respectable orthodox manner. Rather, they come at it sideways, or sneak up from behind, trying to surprise it into revealing something unexpected or even controversial. Inevitably, it's a more subjective approach, with the danger that not everything will catch the imagination of every reader every time. It's a case of chucking a pebble in the pool and hoping that the ripples reach you; if not, move on optimistically to the next pebble.

Ideally I would like this book to be used in several ways:

- to be dipped into at random;
- as a daily / weekly help in reading and reflecting on the Bible;
- as an additional source of ideas for teaching or preaching from the lectionary;
- to be read as part of a service, maybe even instead of a sermon;
- to be used in a group, for reflection or discussion;
- as an inspiration for you to create your own, personal reflections.

The reflections are based on readings taken from Common Worship, Year C (Services and Prayers for the Church of England). You will need to read these first!

Like most people, I guess, I have a magpie hoard of snippets and quotes; gems stolen over the years from I know not where. These I have drawn on with gay abandon and, I fear, no possibility of proper acknowledgement. I can only hope and pray that the worthy authors will be magnanimous, pleased that their words have been an inspiration and may now even inspire a few more: I thank them all.

SHEILA WALKER

Advent

FIRST SUNDAY OF ADVENT

Of Leaves and Branches

Jeremiah 33:4-6; Luke 21:25-36

Down at the recycling centre
the skips are brimming with leaves . . .

First the autumn carnival colours:
pale-moon gold to sunbright yellow,
pink shading to bronze,
crimson creeper to deep purple
of maple and copper beech;
then the greedy gales
stripping the trees of their finery,
tossing it on the ground
in careless, ragged heaps
for children to scuffle
and dutiful gardeners to sweep into sacks.

In the States
they call it still – fortuitously perhaps – the Fall.

But winter trees
stripped of their leafy covering
seem somehow to gain in stature, and dignity;
in the face of this annual baring of the soul
they stand,
without shame, before the Son of Man.

For us
by an accident of geography
Advent comes hard on the heels of the Fall.
'Look at the fig tree, and all the trees:
when they shed their leaves
you can see for yourselves
and know that winter is near.'

And there will be no avoiding winter.
We cannot pick and choose our seasons;
when Christ comes again
will it be the winter of our discontent,
the winter of judgement,
a wintry judgement?
When the leaves of convention are stripped away,
when Adam's fig leaf is gone with the wind –
what of our nakedness, our true self?
In the face of this final baring of the soul
will *we* stand,
without shame, before the Son of Man?

Of course
we prefer, at Advent, to think of Christmas;
we rehearse the beautiful promises
of the first coming, of the Christ child
in all his human helplessness –
however wonderful,
dependent still
on human ministrations,
on mother's milk, on father's skill –
his coming lit by a bright but gentle, purposeful star . . .

The danger
is that babies are sweet.

But Advent
is not for the most part a time to look back to what has been
but a time to look forward
to what is still to come . . .
For every promise, every foretelling
of that first coming of Christ to earth
they say there are *five* that speak
of his second coming; that spell out
his return to earth at the end of the age;
his return as King and as Judge,
his coming lit by explosions of stars,
by the shaking of sun and moon
as the old order is dismantled

and the sea roars its terror or approval . . .
When he comes again
with power and great glory
(and that coming is certain,
and nearer now than when we first believed)
then every eye shall see:
not just a handful of Israeli shepherds
who happened to be in the right place at the right time
but, somehow, everyone, in all the world,
and every knee shall bow . . .

The danger
is that judges are *not* sweet.

Do you remember
the prophets of doom?
Today they would be graffiti artists; then it was sandwich boards
in thick black letters:
'The end of the world is nigh!'
'Prepare to meet thy God!'
People pointed, and sniggered –
the moment's unease quickly buried
by shared reassurance and return to shopping.
We like the carnival colour leaves,
not the stark black lines beneath:
black is too – black;
things can't be that bad, come on,
it's not the end of the world . . .

But one day it will be.

When? We are told only that we do not know when.
Prophecy is not to satisfy our curiosity
but to put us on our guard;
since heaven and earth will pass away
and only the words of Christ remain –
words by which we will all, every one, be judged –
we only know
we must be ready
always ready.

How, ready?

Trees, it would seem, are not only pleasing to the eye,
extremely useful and altogether a brilliant invention
but also a very fruitful source of imagery;
for when the chips are down
and the leaves whipped off
we see among the bare branches
a Branch –
a shoot from the stump of Jesse,
a branch growing out of his roots,
a branch sprouted from the tree of David –
a branch that shall be called
'the Lord our Righteousness'

and he calls us
to be grafted into him
to allow, with overwhelming relief and gratitude,
that only his righteousness can cover our shame;
and he who calls us
is both branch and child, King and judge:
Jesus Christ
whose promise is sure, that
no one whose hope is in him
will ever be put to shame
but will stand, unashamed
before the Son of Man

in the spring of our resurrection,
robed in his righteousness
with the luminous green leaves of the Tree of Life
offered for our healing,
and the healing of the nations.

For those, then, who are found in Christ
there is everything to look forward to:
Advent is a time of adventure, expectation of
wrongs righted
wounds healed

burdens lifted
pains eased.
Judgement, yes – but of the building of our lives:
scrap metal, or gold?
Salvation by the skin of our teeth,
or heaped with rewards?
But salvation itself is assured,
for the gates of heaven stand always open
to the Lord our Righteousness . . .

But for those who fail to recognise
their baseless arrogance –
the wise in their own eyes –
Advent is a time of misadventure, expectation of
wrongs exposed
'expertise' confounded
paradise lost
pride wounded.
Judgement, yes –

unless
we who watch our own lives
watch also that we tell *them* the truth,
the *whole* truth
of the One
who was, and who is, and who is to come.

SECOND SUNDAY OF ADVENT

Stress and Survival

Malachi 3:1-4; Luke 3:1-6

I remember it well,
that long-awaited weekend away . . .
escape from homework and the dire checkout job;
the chance to chill out with all my mates,
a gentle stroll, good food and sunshine
and music, music round the fire
and conversation long into the night
with no thought for tomorrow because it would be out of my hands,
all down to my adored youth leader,
so I could relax;

I could hardly wait for the day to come.

I remember it well,
that long-awaited weekend away . . .
learning long passages of Scripture and reciting them
at four in the morning,
being put in a team with people I didn't know;
rucksack cutting my shoulders as I climbed to 3000 feet,
plastic bags over my boots to keep out the river and the rain –
the only food the packs I rehydrated; the only music
everybody snoring; the only conversation
a few well-chosen words about our adored youth leader;

I could hardly wait for the days to end.

But, all these years later, I remember it *well* –
I grumbled, but I grew
and learned to outgrow grumbling,
because it was a punishable offence;
I struggled, but survived
and learned that weakness shared puts paid to arrogance;

I said 'I can't . . .' but I did
and learned that faith in God *is* confidence
and perhaps, just perhaps that adored youth leader
knew what he was doing, putting his reputation on the line.

And now, as we read of the coming of the Lord
can we hardly wait for that day to come?
A day, we say, when questions will be answered,
a day when truth will be justified,
a day when every tear will be wiped away
as we rejoin those we love who have died;
yes! a day to anticipate, a day to celebrate
with no thought for tomorrow, because it will be out of our hands,
all down to our adored Saviour
so we can relax . . .

Not so fast!
What you speak of is the new Jerusalem,
the new heaven and the new earth,
the new dawn breaking after the darkness,
the day of *darkness* which is the day of the Lord; the day
when we are weighed in the balance and found wanting
when we are tested for impurity and found in need of much refining
when we are inspected and found unprepared
when we are scanned for sin and found in need of much repentance.
When the only similarity to my longed-for weekend break
seems to be the fire

and judgement starts with the household of God.

Will we survive the day of his coming?
For he will be like a refiner's fire, turning up the heat
    under all hypocrisy,
  like Fuller's soap, bleaching the stains
    from our guilty consciences;
  like a tornado, overturning the tables
    in our Temple –
  like the final watershed, dividing
    sheep from goats;

as judgement starts with the household of God

so he came at a time when not one but two were High Priest:
Annas, duly appointed under the Jewish law
and Caiaphas, puppet of Rome, keeping an eye, curbing the power,
giving account to God and to Caesar –
    so he came like a refiner's fire
    and, warming to his subject, taught
    with an authority not seen before
    and the established church got hot under the collar
    as their shortcomings and aberrations
    rose to the surface, to be caught
    in the divine searchlight, skimmed and rejected:
    all that prevented the people from seeing
    his image reflected.

And what of us, here in England today
where the government has the final say
in choosing the head of the 'state' church – can the man escape
the compromise of the office?
    And so he will come to us on that day like a refiner's fire
    and, warming to his subject, judge
    with an authority derived from God
    and we, the established church, will get hot under the collar
    as our shortcomings and aberrations
    rise to the surface, to be caught
    in the divine searchlight, skimmed and rejected
    and we are convicted, having prevented others from seeing
    his image reflected . . .

Must it be so?
Or can we prepare for this, as for any other examination?
It will all depend on our style:
if we are like those who wait till the night before
then swot like mad into the early hours – tough.
Since the date of the exam has not been fixed
now has to be the only day of self-evaluation, of salvation
    now, not tomorrow,
        to ask for a divine hatred of impurity

now, not tomorrow,
  to ask for the fire that tempers steel
now, not tomorrow,
  to ask for an undivided heart
now, not tomorrow,
  to ask for the blood of Christ, that bleaches clean.

Everything that is hidden
will on that day be shouted from the rooftops;
is it not, then, better that I face the pain, the stress
the trial and the testing *now,*
suppress nothing, ignore nothing, hide nothing
but ask for it to rise to the surface
and be taken, healed, forgiven?

So that on that day
there is no unfinished business;
I will have been stripped of all attempts at concealment, all pretence,
all defence,

and will survive: will stand
accepted, thanks to the one who stands beside me, covering me
with his grace and righteousness –
my adored Saviour.

THIRD SUNDAY OF ADVENT

Joy Riding

Zephaniah 3:14-20; Isaiah 12:2-6; Philippians 4:4-7

There *is* joy,
a hitch-hiker standing at the side of the road,
waving, but I am travelling too fast:
by the time my conscience, or my heart
is stirred, I have passed
the point of no return.

I sometimes see the flashy, the boldly dressed
or undressed; I see *thrill,*
exhilaration, sometimes even
ecstasy (with or without a pill):
these I have taken for a ride
– or is it vice versa?

I see, too, *happiness,*
and *contentment,* mature in years,
at peace with the world
and each other: these old dears,
too, I have on occasion picked up
and taken home;

I have also found *pleasure,*
in all manner of guises;
and at certain times, especially
in the football season, *frenzy* rises:
but such seek to accompany me only
to the next service station;

but *joy* – I was not expecting her
to be so soberly dressed,
so quiet; never intrusive or insistent –

so much so that I missed
her gentle request – it was more like an offer –
to come with me all the way.

But as I journeyed, thirst
overtook me: body, and soul and spirit
parched, arid, dry; I stopped,
searched, and found the wells of salvation
and, as I reached to draw water
saw joy standing by.

'Who are you?' I asked.
'I would like to know you . . .'
'This is my home,' she replied;
'I am the child of salvation; and as you drink
deep, so I will show you
the nature of joy.

'Drink deep of the cup of salvation:
be still, and know the delight
of the Lord in you, his child:
know he receives you as you are,
precious in his sight
– in such acceptance, know joy!

'Drink deep of the cup of salvation:
know that the shadows from the past
can all be driven away –
disappointment, and failure, and sin,
all can be redeemed, forgiven
– in such freedom, know joy!

'Drink deep of the cup of salvation:
know you need never fear;
the Lord has promised
to give you his peace; never
will you be alone: always he is near
– in such safety, know joy!

'Drink deep of the cup of salvation:
know that you are no longer adrift
in an aimless, tumultuous world
but are part of God's story
and he is bringing you swiftly home
– in such belonging, know joy!

'Drink deep of the cup of salvation:
know that the Lord of creation
is making all things new –
restoring his image in you, his child,
restoring his just and peaceful rule
– in such re-creation, know joy!

'As you come to the wells of salvation
take time, as you draw your water
to see my reflection in it
and as you drink, give me
a personal invitation:
let me in!

'And the more you let me into your life
the more you will also need
to let me out:
I will dance on your doubt,
I will dance in your heart and your eyes,
I will free you to sing and shout,

'to worship the Lord your God
with all of your heart and soul
and none of your inhibitions;
this is your gift: this is your whole
intent, this is your strength
and this is his due . . .

'It is true, I am not always loud;
you saw me first in my sober dress
for when it is dark

I will speak encouraging words
of certain hope, in gentleness,
in confidence and quiet trust . . .

'Know me, child of the light,
know me in riches or rags,
know me in grief or in celebration,
know me by day and by night
for I am your light shadow;
I am the child of salvation.'

We stood and talked by the well;
I wanted to hold her fast
but she gently shook her head
and I watched in dismay
as she slipped away down the shaft:
'You know where to find me,' she said.

FOURTH SUNDAY OF ADVENT

Pregnant Pause

Luke 1:39-45 (55)

There's nothing like pregnancy for demonstrating
that waiting is no game . . .

Getting started, for a start: falling pregnant
may well not be as easy as falling off a log;
I must learn to hush my hopes,
refuse to let my imagination run riot,
check my eager-beaver expectation –
as if . . . !
As if it were possible to soften the blow
as the months go by, as the years go by
and I do not know how to guard my heart from hardening
or my spirit from sinking in quiet despair.

Elizabeth knew, she must have asked
'Is it me? Is it him? Are we sinful, incompetent, sick
or is it just a matter of time?
How will it end?'
That is the hardest – *never knowing how it will end,*
waiting, wondering how to live between all and nothing.

Waiting is no game,
rather self-induced torture of nerves and faith
on the slow rack of time.

But now – it's been confirmed,
the tests are positive, even against all the odds
(and you couldn't have much greater odds than they did,
the cousins, what with Elizabeth's age,
and Mary's virginity).

But even now, I must not count my chickens:
those early months are precarious –
the embryo may not be firmly established;
neither, then, can I establish my heart
or allow it to sing too loud –
not yet: still I must wait, and wonder, balancing joy and dread
until the various hazards are passed
and I can begin to tell my friends the news,
the way it is, the due date –
but always as a likelihood,
never a fait accompli,

for there is yet more waiting and wondering
always more waiting
with its own bellyful of possible outcomes.

But for Mary and her cousin – was it so
or, because the angel had spoken, were they spared
that white-water raft of uncertainty?
For the plan of God can surely never miscarry.

But *I* did not hear the voice of the angel
when this new thing first stirred inside me: I heard
only the ache of a man and a woman
and assumed the silent assent of God to come to this moment, yes:
but after this, no promises . . .

so, when the scan shows signs of abnormality, I can only panic
and wait, wonder, wait
and it's certainly no game.

I bet Elizabeth and Mary would have been glad
not to have had the very mixed blessing of scans –
not that they needed them; they'd have known enough,
known that nothing could be wrong;
it was out of their hands, all in the hands of God
(and the finest scanner would never show that abnormal filling with all the
Holy Spirit's fullness while still in utero . . .).

But me – I have been told too much, and too little –
I can only wait, and wonder, the weight of foreboding
grounding every prayer my voice prays
while my mind plays and replays
every scenario from misery to miracle.

And when this scare, too, has passed
and I have allowed myself to rejoice in the miracle,
still I envy those cousins, for whom the waiting
could be a time of unchallenged joy
whilst I cannot be sure that there may not be a need,
but no assurance of, more miracles.

And now, when the child is due,
there is still more waiting; for God, it seems
has not delivered his promises;
they are overdue, and I am impatient and heavy,
excitement lost in the aching need for it all to be over.

But they, they could receive the events,
and the non-events of each day with equal peace;
Mary saying 'yes' without misgiving
to the long, uncomfortable ride to Bethlehem,
not waiting and wondering, but living, trusting God's time.

And when that time comes,
and the pain is more than I dreamed, more, surely, than I can bear
and the child is a long time coming, too long –
what is wrong? There must be something wrong, even now
I know it can all go wrong, and all this waiting will be,
or will seem to be,
for nothing.

And when the child is born,
even then my relief and joy is suddenly tempered, knowing that still
I must wait to see
just what it is that God has birthed in me

for even when angels speak, there is no guarantee
that *all* will live happily ever after;
that the children of promise will not be strange and wild
and die a cruel and seemingly premature death.
Did the cousins, for all their blessedness,
rejoice in God their Saviour to the bitter end?

I guess
the answer must be yes
and no: the angel gave them a head start but, like me,
they were only human, needing to learn the hard way:
    to wait, without wondering about all the things that happened before
    and what might have been,
    to wait, without wondering about all that tomorrow
    may, or may not hold in store;
    to wait, in the settled knowledge
    that God is fulfilling this present moment without haste or delay;
    to trust the power of God against the odds
    to trust the word of God in the war of words
    to trust the love of God in the midst of pain.

Wait . . . what is the seed that God is sowing in you and me?
What is the purpose that God is growing in you and me?
Encourage me, and I will encourage you
to stand in wonder, that whether the angel speaks or not,
God is true.

Christmas

CHRISTMAS DAY

Wordpower

John 1:1-14; [Genesis 1:1-27]

Just imagine if,
every time you commanded 'coat hanger'
or 'caterpillar'
one came into being;

every time you mentioned 'mousetrap'
or 'motorway'
one more materialised;

every time you spoke of 'sycamore'
or 'submarine'
another surfaced.

But in the beginning it was just so:
the word of God took on a life of its own
and became light, and dark
land, and sea
fish, flesh, fowl:
no sooner said than done!

Just as well he knew when to stop
or we'd be stuck in the stuff of a zany, runaway children's book
instead of a centred, sufficient world.

But just imagine the power of that word
to command thought to thicken,
to take on form and weight;
to spin an idea into threads
of colour and shape
and set it weaving, dancing;
to see in his mind's eye

a million possibilities
and choose them all.

Just imagine the power of that word
in the beginning:
and that it did all begin
with – the word,
the smallest meaningful unit of speech:
meaningful,
not just a noise, a noisy big bang
but a *word,* with purpose and meaning
to give *us* purpose and meaning.

A word that spoke volumes
in a week that changed the world
from nothingness to paradise
(however long that week lasted,
and by whatever process those words materialised:
whatever! They were divine, creative words –
to God be the glory!)

And what is this?
'The Word became flesh, and dwelt among us . . .'
A date marked on the cosmic calendar
when the Word that commanded worlds reinvents itself,
erupting into the middle of history as an inarticulate baby,

when the everywhere God whom, as Solomon said,
even the highest heaven of heavens
could not contain, deigned
not to presence himself in a temple, but to fit
into a manger,

when the God who is beyond naming, YHWH, I AM
who I AM, and I will be who I will be,
indescribable, Word beyond words, agrees
to be called Jesus, Emmanuel
God with us,

this is grace.

And what is this?
'The Word became flesh, and dwelt among us . . .'
A life lived in an Arab land, under Roman rule
when a carpenter's son taught his teachers
how the law and the prophets dovetailed
into the Kingdom of God . . .

when a travelling preacher man
painted a revolutionary portrait:
a saviour coming as suffering servant,
confounding the Jewish assumptions
about the Messiah . . .

when the one called the Son of God
defined both the nature of God
and of the word 'love',
when he laid down his life in order to save
whoever believes,

this is truth.

'The Word became flesh, and dwelt among us,
full of grace and truth.'

Then, as now, most did not know him;
now, as then, most do not know him.

For what is this?
The Word has come
but we answer him by bemoaning our lack of energy,
time and money to meet all the expectations
of this annual feast of Mammon;
we sing of peace on earth and revile our relations;

Almighty God has come
but we are busy putting things in boxes,
tying them up and sticking on labels;
there used to be a largish box for God, but I think
it got used for Aunt Mabel;

the Name above all names has come
but he's not on our Christmas list, or rather, our Xmas list
for although we're definitely up for a celebration
we're not sure any more about Christ
so we'll call it X – the unknown designation,

and this is Christmas??

No, Lord;
I fear
it is a travesty, an unholy mixture.
I fear
you may become weary of your word falling on deaf ears
and decide to go away for Christmas.
I fear
a silent night.

Lord,
speak your word again and create in me a spark of joy,
speak your word again and create in me a song of faith,
speak your word again and create in me a soul ablaze
with the grace and truth
of Christmas.

FIRST SUNDAY OF CHRISTMAS

Boy Wonder

1 Samuel 2:18-20, 26

Oh boy,
you can just see the headlines if it happened today:
'Mother abandons child of three;
doctors to look into her mental stability.'
'Boarding school at three?
It's too young!' says top educationalist.
'Priest accused of child abuse
claims he had "duty of care"'.
'Unnatural upbringing will damage child for life'
declares leading psychologist.

Oh Lord, don't you love it when all the experts turn out to be wrong?

Samuel,
God heard
heard your mother's prayer,
silent cry of despair from a soul barren of expectation
but faithful still to serve her Lord.
God heard
heard your mother's longing
to conceive, not for her own sake or reputation
but to give back to her Lord.
God heard
heard your mother's constancy
true to her word, trusting, unwavering in dedication
and gave her the desire of her heart:
Samuel.

And she sang; Hannah,
your mother, sang to her Lord,
sang to celebrate the child he would give and she would give back;

sang the song that her Lord's own mother, Mary, would find
a thousand years later
to celebrate the child he would himself become
and she would give back:
Magnificat
'My soul exults in the Lord, my spirit rejoices in God my Saviour.'

Oh Lord, don't you love it when all the experts turn out to be wrong?

Wrong about Samuel,
when they walked into the temple at Shiloh and said
'What's that kid doing here, for heaven's sake?
He should be playing with clay, and learning to count sheep
and generally causing delight and despair to his mother . . .'

But no: here is a child of three or four
ministering to the Lord,
who knows how?
Looking to imitate Eli
in dress, and discernment, and diligence.
Didn't he cry for his mother at night?
Didn't he play hopscotch on the paving stones of the temple court?
Didn't he throw a tantrum when Eli laid down the law?
Who knows now . . .
but no reason to suppose
he was some pale childhood paragon of all virtues – rather
a normal small boy, who grows in virtue, grows wise
by mastering the rough ground
and finding God in the enterprise.

And no: here is a mother who in no way
abandoned her child; surely never forgot her Samuel,
heard by God
every tug of the needle through cloth
the pricking of tears
as she stitched her prayer, year by year,
into the little robe, a little larger each year;
but how much larger? Might he have had an illness
which thinned him, laid him low,

or a surge of growing, of gangly legs and arms?
Better make the hem deep, allow for an extra fold of stuff.
How much, how many moments she missed:
yet would not have missed, for all the world –
the getting, and the giving of this special gift.

And how was it for her, each year
and for Elkanah, the husband who loved her, trusted her
to make the right decision for his boy –
how was it for them, as they went to make their sacrifice
not just of another animal, that was the easy part,
however much it cost –
but of their son, again and again,
again to treat their eyes, to feel their heart
leap with pride and longing –
again, almost before hands have touched,
to let go . . .

And Samuel,
did he stand at the window, watching for them to come?
Did he stand at the window, watching them as they went,
looking back, or not looking back,
waving, or not waving,
blinking through tears of sorrow, or of joy?
Did it get easier, or harder?

No matter! Because of, or in spite of it all,
Samuel grew in the presence of the Lord . . .

Oh Lord, don't you love it when all the experts turn out to be wrong?

Wonder of wonders,
Samuel grew to be one of the greatest of Israel's heroes,
judge and king-maker, prophet and priest;
son who would make any mother proud,
servant with whom any Lord would be pleased.

So, do it your way, Lord! *You* are the expert . . .

And what of *my* child,
my grandchild, my neighbour's child of three or four –
might they, too, be ministering to the Lord?
Who is found for *them* to imitate?
Am I too quick to relegate them to the crèche,
out of sight, out of mind, never mind what they're doing,
as long as they're quiet?
But something is going on between them and God:
what? Could it be something special?
Yes; always.

Help me to listen, Lord,
not to the experts, who would pattern us
according to the latest supposed wisdom,
but to you
who, with every new creation, break the mould.

Do it your way, Lord:
you are *the* expert.

SECOND SUNDAY OF CHRISTMAS

Borrowed Glory?

Ephesians 1:3-14

A heavyweight among words,
this *glory;*
and one we hesitate to use
finding, perhaps, little to be worthy of it
outside of God
and for most of us
most of God
is outside of our experience

and, as our experience of glory fades,
so the word is dumbed down
and the crown of glory
goes to the small-town carnival queen.

But oh! How are such mighty words fallen!
Glory . . . God's very self revealed
tempestuously
in cloud and storm and fire,
dazzlingly
in Christ, sunburst upon the world,
weightily
in Gethsemane and Golgotha,
triumphantly
in risen, everlasting splendour.

Yahweh, glory of your people Israel
and father of our Emmanuel,
Jesus, glory of your new Israel:
even us, your Church.

For we were not always such strangers to glory,
made, as we were, in the image of God;

once the mere sight of Adam and Eve
would have dazzled God with his own brilliance,
stars of Eden outshining the stars of heaven.
But no more,
since they sought to take to themselves the glory of God
they, and we their descendants wander alone, inglorious:
for *he* is the Lord;
his glory he will not give to another.
No substitutes.
No borrowed glory.

How we need to discover again,
glory belongs to God.
How we need to discover again
that our whole life's work
is to gaze on that glory
and wonder, and worship, blissfully unaware
that as we gaze, as we wonder, as we worship
so we reflect the glory
we can neither beg, borrow nor steal.

How we need to discover again
the grace of the glory of God;
that it is all of him, and nothing of us –
the choosing, before we were born
before the world was born:
for what?
To be holy and blameless before him:
unblemished, untarnished mirror,
no foxing,
reflecting unhindered his pure image,
so all can see
and discover again, in a human face, glory –
the glory of the grace of God.

It is all of him, and nothing of us,
the provision of polish and soft cloth
to clean up the mirror:
for what?

To be to the praise of his glory:
no holding back, no hesitation,
no keeping the credit,
naming in all things *his* hand
so all can see
and discover again, in a human face, glory –
the glory of the grace of God.

But *do* we name him, give him glory?
Was that meeting chance, coincidence
or the weaving of God?
Was the healing a normal occurrence
or an answer to prayer?
Was the sunset a splendid accident of nature
or a new work from the divine portfolio?
What will we say?
Will we take it all for granted
and say nothing?
Will we rate our own central role or skill
and sneak the credit?
Or will we faithfully give God the glory
and risk the rebuff?

We say it on Sunday:
Yours is the kingdom, the power *and the glory* –
but on Monday?
How will the world know that we live for him,
or glimpse the edge of God
if our words as well as our works
do not reflect his glory?
Is that why, in our town,
we see so little sign of the power of God?
Because we'd only explain it away
in Nazarene unbelief
instead of applauding it for all we're worth,
for all it's worth, for all he's worth –
like Paul, who was so overwhelmed
by the endless grace of the glory of God
that he couldn't stop,

couldn't bear to stop worshipping God
in that tumbling, superlative, seemingly endless sentence of praise . . .

To live to the praise of his glory –
that is why I am here;
to push the limits
of my understanding, and find there is more,
always more of the grace of God;
more heavenly riches in Christ
more blessing relayed by the Spirit;

as I open my eyes
to see the glory of God
he will everywhere meet my gaze;
as I open my mouth
to declare the glory of God;
he will fill it with praise . . .

As I see, and speak out
to God be the glory!
so I become whole, and
so will others see, and speak out in turn
to God be the glory!
and find that their life's goal, their lives,
and words will be redeemed:

To God be the glory!

Epiphany

World Map

Isaiah 60:1-6; Psalm 72:(1-9), 10-15; Ephesians 3:1-12

I often wish I could go back to school
and retake all those subjects I found boring,
or was too young to appreciate;
history seemed to hop across the centuries,
a mish-mash of wars and dates
with no rhyme or reason, no thread.
The same with geography: so many names
of mountains and volcanoes
that might have come from anywhere,
sounding merely foreign; lists
of imports and exports, copper, wool,
diamonds, oil, rubber, tea –
but so what?

I did love the maps, though:
maps with red dots for population
maps with black dots for mineral resources
maps with green dots for pasture land
maps with blue arrows for trade routes
maps with dotted lines for bridleways
maps with hatching for deforestation
and maps with rainbow colours
for all the countries of the world:
do you remember, pink for the British Empire?
But so what?

What, in all this, is significant?
If *God* were to make a map, now,
a projection, what would it look like?
Given the geography,
what history would inform his choice

of boundaries? Which colour felt-tip
for which movement
of which peoples?

Doubtless
the Middle East provides the focal point;
the oldest maps (if such existed) showing
a multi-coloured flurry of activity,
ebbing and flowing
towards Palestine
with a bright gold x marking the spot
for Zion, Jerusalem, city of God . . .

But then, two thousand or so years ago,
the map undergoes a dramatic change:
a secret has been told,
a mystery revealed
and the golden glow of God
filters across the map as the star rises
and the news spreads:

> 'Salvation is not for the Jews alone
> but for *all* who believe
> so GO for gold! Colour me
> a whole, beautiful world!'

And so God's map will look to him
like the church, the body of Christ, his Son . . .
like a slow-motion picture
as each new believer,
each new gold dot
helps build the body
and redraw the map . . .

now, the body propelled from Zion by persecution
but with heart beating
and arms reaching out
to Turkey, Greece, the Roman Empire
and feet following;
and more gold dots appear, and the body grows
in the wake of Paul, apostle to the Gentiles

but now, in those lands, rival religions
and decadence – gold faded and overlaid . . .

And the body based in Western Europe
with heart beating
and arms reaching out
to Africa, Asia, the world
and feet following;
and more gold dots appear, and the body grows
in the wake of a wave of Western missions

but now, in Europe only the outward form,
meaningless, lifeless dots . . .

And the body sprawls in the south,
often poor, sometimes dying of Aids
but with heart beating
and arms reaching out
to the 'hollow men' of Europe,
and feet following;
and will more gold dots appear, and the body grow again
as the Third World comes to our aid?

The map of God will take, always
the contour of the body of Christ, his Son,
changing, moving, shifting shape in order to touch
the furthermost parts of the earth:
a foot in Finland to stand on tiptoe
and reach right into the Arctic Circle;
and now, kneel for a moment in Niger
to stretch out and quench the thirst
of the desert tribes
or step across to the Solomon Isles
to plead with Pacific peoples . . .
Changing, moving, shifting
but always the shape
of the body of Christ, his Son

hanging a light in every angle of sky
so that always, wise men will see and follow.

And who is more likely to appear
on God's map, I wonder: a Chinese peasant,
who one night has a vision of Jesus,
or Genghis Khan, with one of the greatest empires ever?

Who is more likely to appear
on God's map: Columbus sailing the seven seas
or two elderly ladies,
praying away in the Hebrides?

Who is more likely to appear
on God's map: the crowned heads of Europe
or the Salvation band playing carols
on London's Underground?

God's map,
always the shape
of the body of Christ, his Son,
the body of Christ, his true church:
all those, but only those who are *in Christ,*
part of his body,
appear
on the world's most significant map.

Am I here?
am I one of those gold dots?
part of that heart beating,
part of those arms reaching out,
part of those feet following?
put me on your map, Lord,
or I am
history.

FIRST SUNDAY OF EPIPHANY (BAPTISM OF CHRIST)

War on Terror

Isaiah 43:1-7; Psalm 29

The psalmist, apparently, had no qualms
about seeing the Lord as the power behind the thunderstorm
that raged through the land of Israel,
from Lebanon right down to the desert of Kadesh.

Are we, then, to understand
that he is also the power behind the tsunami
that flattened the Asian coasts?
The typhoon that whipped the South China Sea?
The earthquakes which, with increasing frequency,
reduce communities to rubble?
The hurricanes which make matchwood
of homes and history?

How are we then to understand your promise, Lord,
that when we pass through the rivers
they will not sweep over us,
when we walk through the fire,
we will not be burned?
To be sure, this was a word through Isaiah to Israel
but we who belong to you, are we not the new Israel?

How are we then to understand these terrors, Lord?
Have you merely set in motion a world
where winds and waves are free to blow, or throw their weight around –
or do you, as in the days of Noah, decide
when, and where, and why, to lift your restraining hand?
Climate change threatens.
How firmly, Lord, do you hold the balance of nature?

And are we, then, to understand
that you also delimit the actions of men?

Prompting the friends or foes of Israel
to play their part in your people's story –
but if that was true of Cyrus,
what of Hitler?

We live in an age of 'global war on terror'
when it seems there is no rhyme nor reason,
no limit to who may come under fire
no knowing where they will strike next
no clearly defined objective to meet
no means of dealing with those who do not fear death,
who belong to no one nation
who form no one network
who work to no one pattern:
whose one aim
is to terrorise,
destabilise . . .
Climate change threatens,
for *their* aim is to create a climate of fear.

And how we play into their hands
when the media fan the flames,
keeping the story alive for months,
putting words in the mouth of the young mum,
'Well, yes, I *am* afraid now to let the children go out to play'
putting words in the mouth of the landlord
'Well, yes, I *am* afraid now of having a foreign tenant'
putting words in the mouth of the young Muslim
'Well, yes, I *am* afraid now of bullying and discrimination . . .'

If only
one day they interviewed someone who said
'No! I'm not afraid; the Lord tells me not to fear,
for he has redeemed me, and loves me.
He has called me by name; I am his.
The Lord gives strength to his people, blesses his people with peace.
Climate change?
Nothing can change the climate of the love of God which holds me.

'No! I'm not afraid; I will build my sea-wall
and I will not build on the flood plain or the fault line;
I will cut down on my use of energy and resources
and I will not cut down too many trees:
but at the end of the day,
when earth, air, fire and water –
the elemental energies of God –
are set free,
I don't stand a chance . . .
But I am not afraid:
knowing that death will come, today,
tomorrow, somehow, somewhere
and that Christ will bring me, safe, to the other side –
these terrors have no power in me.

'No! I'm not afraid: I will watch for unattended packages
and I will not travel to a war zone;
I'll preach equality, respect and understanding
and I will not listen to gossip and prejudice:
but at the end of the day
no security system on earth
can protect me
against the one with a cause
for which he or she is not afraid to die:
I don't stand a chance.
But I am not afraid:
knowing that death will come, today,
tomorrow, somehow, somewhere
and that Christ will bring me, safe, to the other side –
these terrors have no power in me.'

When world leaders talk about waging war on terror
they surely mean
terrorism:
and they will not win it,
ever.
They will never control every chemical substance,
every weapon, every computer hacker:

least of all, the explosive, sinful
deceitful human heart.

But the war on terror,
yes, that can be won:
not by greater national security,
international cooperation, global warnings,
but by you and me, by every man and woman in the street:
the paddy field, factory or store –
Yes! This is true democracy: in the end
it is we who, by the grace of God, have the greatest power,
the only power to win this war,

refusing to be terrorised,
destabilised,
holding that vital piece of intelligence:
that the war between good and evil
has already been won.
Fearing the Lord himself, I need not fear
whatever else his hand allows,
whatever instruments of judgement and salvation.

The Lord reigns
and by his grace
I am his.

SECOND SUNDAY OF EPIPHANY

Delight

Isaiah 62:1-5; Psalm 36:5-10

Delight –
it's there, in the word,
a word like a dark plum, so ripe, so heavy
that it must surely fall;
a word like a sleeping child, so still, so trusting
that hearts turn over –
a word redolent with contentment
        that what was sown comes to maturity
        but also with surprise
        that it so exceeds expectation.

Delight –
a word, I am so afraid,
that is likely to fall out of circulation
taking *time*, as it does,
        time to contemplate,
        time to appreciate
        time to love.
In an age that prides itself on travelling in the fast lane,
delight
leans its elbows on the farm gate
and watches the world go by.
Delight
is the unexpected feel of solid ground beneath my feet,
when suddenly I am one with the world
and think that, yes, in the creation of God
I have glimpsed God
and tingle with the wonder of him.

It must be great to be God,
and have all the time in the world

or rather, be beyond all the times of the world;
to have time to delight, again,
at the curls of new bracken, at the same time
delight in a broken marriage healed, at the same time
delight in a child born into the world, at the same time
delight in a man born again into his kingdom, at the same time
delight in – me?

I hardly dare believe –
it seems almost shocking –
that God himself should delight in *me*:
surely he knows me too well?

Or is it that I don't know *him* well enough,
well enough to know that he sees me, like Zion,
destined for glory,
destined to be a trophy, held high,
destined for marriage as part of the bride of Christ,
well enough to know that the love of God will never let go
of his destiny's child,
well enough to know that he is restoring me
so graciously
so utterly
so delightfully.

Delight,
the ardent love of God
discerned in tranquillity.

God's delight in me is unique,
complete;
there is no one quite like me,
no one else he can delight in
as he delights in me.
It is – unbelievably –
up close and personal; I am
so precious
so humbled
so – glad.

It must be great to be God,
and have a heart for the whole world;
to take delight not only in me
and you, and you, and you
but in what we should be together:
for Eden, original place of delight,
was not for Adam alone.
And so the heart of God is not simply for *me*
but for *us*; he calls for
    the restoration of a *city*
    the redemption of a *people*
    the equipping of a *body*.
Only as I find my feet
    as a citizen of the city
    numbered with the saints,
    a vital cell in the body,
will I be – completely – me
and will his delight
be complete.

Lord,
I so want to take a leaf from your book, to
learn to be a delight-full person
learn to take delight
learn to give delight
learn to spark delight in you.

If you can delight in me, for all my faults and failings
may I learn to take time
to take delight
in every good thing you have placed in my life,
in every good thing you have placed in every person
who touches my life;
such time will never be wasted
as the sunshine of delight
teases the tight buds of my love into flower.

If you can delight in the world, for all its faults and failings
may I learn to take time

to give delight
to those who take a major part in my life
and those who make up the backdrop –
for all are sent from you;
such time will never be wasted
as the sunshine of delight
teases the tight buds of their love into flower.

If you can delight in your church, for all its faults and failings,
may I learn to take time
to spark delight
in the God who takes the unruly urchin from the street
and commits himself to her transformation
into the bride of Christ;
such time will never be wasted
as the sunshine of delight
teases the tight buds of our love for him, and each other, into flower.

Delight,
the secret weapon of God,
dealing with our defences, disarming;

delight,
the silent song of praise,
the heart kneeling before his majesty;

delight,
the ardent love of God
discerned in tranquillity.

THIRD SUNDAY OF EPIPHANY

Wise in Our Own Eyes

Nehemiah 8:1-3, 5, 6, 8-10

And all the Israelite people,
all who could understand,
assembled as one man (all right, person,
if you *will* be politically correct –
a political and sociological miracle, anyway).
You just can't imagine it today:
I mean, what,
if anything, would mobilise
everyone?

Royal wedding? Pretty good, apart from the republicans . . .
World cup match? Not so many wives, perhaps . . .
Anti-war protest? Getting a bit active, here . . .
General election? Don't be funny!

We *are* a funny lot, though:
in the age of the *United* Nations,
the European *Union*
and *universal* human rights
too much togetherness is still taboo
too much commitment suspect;
let's keep to dialogue, and consultations
for I am not the same as you . . .

Diversity and tolerance
are king and queen
(except that we do have a somewhat ambivalent attitude
towards the monarchy, see above).

Of course, we are now three generations who,
by and large, have not seen war.

Must it be for ever true
that only war, natural or unnatural disaster
will draw and bind us together, have us acting as one?
That here, in its absence, we have become
a collection of individuals held loosely together
by a mark on a passport, a diminishing reticence
a taste for Mastermind
and warm beer?

Hard to imagine how we,
with our small enthusiasms,
could ever have mustered with such anticipation
for *anything,*
least of all to listen, all ears
to a book of rules
purporting to be
from *God* ?!

And, more amazing still,
it would seem those Israelites actually *asked* for it:
that their time in that foreign land of Babylon –
that spell in Iraq
when they found it so hard to sing their songs,
the songs of Zion, to keep their cultural identity –
that time of exile
made its mark
made them realise
made them appreciate
all that they had taken so lightly,
all that they had spurned:
the goodness of God, the good sense of God,
the care and the favour of God.
And so those exiles returned
to their senses, rightly
contritely
learning again the received wisdom
of the God of their fathers.

And Ezra read to them from daybreak to noon:
five, six hours? And they, hanging

on his every word.
And what is our attention span –
three or four hours for a blockbuster movie
(with CGI and stereo sound)
a couple of hours for a rugby match
but a red card for the preacher found
in breach of the ten-minute rule.

Could even God himself arrest our jaded senses
(assuming, for a moment,
we believed in him?)
Could he have us on our feet,
one minute cheering, waving with that enthusiasm
usually reserved for winning goals
and the next, prostrated – no,
not sunning ourselves on a beach
but seeking the Son of God
for the saving of our souls?

Could it happen?
Could it be that, together, we will ever again say
This is it!
This is the pearl of great price,
this is the treasure for which we will sell everything else;
no more channel-hopping, internet shopping:
here and here alone is the way, the truth and the life!

Are we still a people who can weep
for the sheer beauty of truth
and for our own shortcomings
or are we dulled, desensitised,
deprived by too much choice
of the power to choose?

We have made our minor choices into an art form,
a lifestyle,
going online to surf the superstore aisles,
choosing this week the short or long grain, brown,

basmati or risotto rice,
thumbing the Argos catalogue for this month's treat,
waiting for the Lottery results,
selecting or deselecting from the charts,
encapsulating on the iPod this week's self.

But what of the major choices –
the ones that summon both heights and depths
the full measure of our emotions,
that lay us bare to ridicule from lesser men;
the ones that fix our course,
come what may; that dare, even,
to exclude?
Of these, we seem to have become
morbidly wary
preferring our small, inconsequential pleasures
to the risky exhilaration
of the joy of the Lord.

Where, oh where are the Levites of today –
inspired interpreters
revealers of revelation
iconic weavers of received wisdom?

Received wisdom?
Oh, but that flies in the face
of our taste for the latest;
yesterday is long superseded,
today is only just OK,
tomorrow is the new black!
Sack the pundits, they're no longer needed:
we prefer to be wise
in our own eyes.

Weep for us.

FOURTH SUNDAY OF EPIPHANY

Fallen in Love

1 Corinthians 13:1-13

Fallen in love
has to be one of the stupidest phrases in the world.

Take *fall* for a start:
according to my dictionary it means
'to descend by the force of gravity from a higher to a lower place'
'to collapse to the ground, especially in pieces'
'to become less in quality'.

Is this really what we meant to say about the love of our lives?

And what about *in love?*
Is love, then, a state into which I can stumble
like unexpectedly soft heather at the foot of a cliff,
moonlight on roses,
a warm sea
or even a man-trap set for the unwary?

We speak as though it is – out there, somewhere,
if only we could find it.

However stupid it may be
I think, though
that we will continue
to say that we have *fallen in love*
because it masquerades
as something that happens to us, involuntary,
something over which we have little control,
for which we therefore bear little responsibility;
and wouldn't we all like to find ourselves
written into that fairy tale, where *falling in love*
leads to *happily ever after?*

Well, all I can say is,
if that's the myth you want to perpetuate,
don't read 1 Corinthians 13 at your wedding
because Paul is talking about something
completely different.

Love is *not*
a feeling
a state
an obsession
or a chemical reaction;
it is not a justification for anything from adultery to euthanasia.

Love is *not*
a romantic poem
a valentine rose
a lingering kiss
or a lofty sentiment;
it is not an excuse for anything from perjury to suicide.

Love is
what love does
when no one is looking;
love is
what love says
when no one is listening;
love is
what love thinks
when no one is knowing.

Love is patient –
Am I patient?
How do you know,
unless you see me, month by month, care for my autistic child
(and how do you know
I am *truly* patient
and not gritting my teeth and screaming inside?)

Love is kind –
Am I kind?

How do you know
unless you see me take my neighbour's rubbish to the tip
(and how do you know
I am *truly* kind
and not trying to earn some heavenly Brownie points?)

Love keeps no record of wrongs –
Am I forgiving?
How do you know
unless you see me kiss and make up
(and how do you know
I am *truly* forgiving
and will not file the offence for future reference?)

No, don't ask Paul to your wedding
unless you're ready to learn
of a love that is, above all,
voluntary,
of a love that does not exist
unless you *will* it, unless *you* create it,
think it, speak it, do it,
irrespective
of feelings,
circumstance,
or reward;
irrespective of the fact that you'll never get it right,
disentangle your motives, never cease to fail –
or fall – in love;

the love that is
what love does
when no one is looking;
the love that is
what love says
when no one is listening;
the love that is
what love thinks
when no one is knowing.

Paul speaks of faith, hope and love:
but what hope is there
of learning such a love as he portrays,
the love that will never fail, that will stand not only
the tantrums and trials of the next days, or months or years
but the fire of that final judgement
when perfect love
tries love?

Was I then wrong to say
that love does not exist unless we create it?
Yes, I was wrong:
we love only because God first loved us,
he who *is* that pure love
uncreated
overflowing
into creation, and into every vessel offered to him.

I fail; he who *is* love never fails;
I fall; he who *is* grace raises me up,
again and again, saying here, give me your heart,
and let me press it close to mine so that my life-blood,
my love, will flow through your veins;
only when you are in me, and I in you
can you truly say that you,
fallen as you are,
are in love.

Ordinary Time

PROPER 1

Seeing, and Partly Seeing

Isaiah 6:1-8 (9-13); 1 Corinthians 15:1-11; Luke 5:1-11

I can well believe that, by default or design,
we use only the merest fraction of our brains;
we hear only the merest fraction of what is actually said;
we see only the merest fraction of what is actually there –
especially when it comes to God.

I remember when a friend of mine –
one of those blasé, been there, seen it, got the T-shirt types –
was completely bowled over by the Taj Mahal:
nothing could prepare you for a sight like that, he said.
How much more, when it comes to God.

It probably doesn't help
that we are getting so good at fabricating fearsomeness;
with all our computer graphics, all our hi-tech gizmos
we can conjure images that plunder our emotions
yet we remain in control: we play God;

but it was surely much more
than a lack of technical know-how, a lack of exposure
to the big screen, to the wonders of *son et lumière*
that floored Isaiah: nothing could have prepared him, ever,
for the sight of God.

Would you see God?
Mind how you answer . . .

Many who have seen God,
in that same moment saw themselves for the first time,
not partly, but wholly,
wholly undone by the holiness of God;

senses urging flight from that consuming fire
yet rooted in dreamlike impotence,
awaiting ruin;
needing to put the Sea of Galilee between them
as if water could quench that fire
or distance alter truth.

Compared with others in my class
I'm not *so* stupid;
compared with others in my office
I'm not *as* careless with my phone calls or expense account;
compared with others in my street
I'm not *too* gossipy;
compared with others in my church
I'm *less* hypocritical;
from this, I have thus far drawn comfort –
but no more.
Before God,
comparing is impertinence, irrelevant; his holiness
reveals my true condition: I am arrested by my sinfulness;
wild creature transfixed in the headlights of the car.

Seeing God is being seen by him
and finding myself exposed
flat on my face
in stunned repentance.

And when I dare to look,
I see that he is coming to meet me,
coming with live coal from his altar
to burn up my idle words;
coming with tears of heavenly joy
over this one sinner who has repented.

Seeing God is being seen by him;
is repenting,
is finding oneself,
forgiven,
refined by his fire, washed clean by his angels' tears.

Would you see God?
Mind how you answer,
for it doesn't stop there . . .
Forgiven,
I am refined for use, fired with purpose,
washed so that others may see him reflected more clearly.

'You have seen, Isaiah – now hear,
hear my word, to go –
go and tell what you know,
go and tell what I will show you,
go, to a people who may be selectively deaf,
go, nonetheless, with my words of grief and glory;
go, and speak my matchless mysteries
and let those who have ears, hear
through the years what my spirit is saying:
go!

'And you, you have seen, Peter – now hear,
hear my word, to come –
come away from your nets
come away from the lapping of your ordered life;
come and put your skills to more eternal use,
come and fish for folk adrift
come, leave everything and follow me
and let those who have ears, hear
through the years what my spirit is saying:
come!

'And you, you have seen, Paul –
you, and several hundred others, you have seen
the risen Christ: now hear,
hear my word, to be changed –
changed from public enemy number one to beloved brother,
changed from wavering disciple to bold martyr,
changed from debauchery to devotion,
changed from one degree of glory to another
with all the joy and agony that change requires;

and let those who have eyes, see
and let those who have ears, hear
through the years what my spirit is saying:
be changed!'

Seeing God is being seen by him,
is repenting,
is finding oneself
forgiven,
refined by his fire, washed clean by his angels' tears
and commissioned
to come
to go
to be changed.

Would you see God?
Mind how you answer . . .

PROPER 2

Break My Heart

Jeremiah 17:5-10; Luke 6:17-26

Excuse me,
do you mind if I break your heart?
All in a good cause, you know:
happiness starts with a broken heart . . .

What? Try telling that
to the girl without a valentine,
the dancer with the twisted spine,
the miner out of work at forty-nine,
the father of four jailed for life for a crime he did not commit!
They will tell me
it's a very long road from heartbreak to happiness
and I am talking through my hat.

Am I? Ask first,
what is happiness?
To the girl – a boyfriend, starry skies and thrills;
to the dancer – health and strength;
to the miner – work and a wage to pay the bills;
to the prisoner – freedom from the cell's length
and the weight of injustice.

Are these happiness?
Desirable, certainly; pleasurable, and a relief, sure:
but is this all that happiness entails
or do we limit the word
by our own limitations?
Is it a matter of where in the world our ship sails,
a matter of family, rainfall and natural resources,
a matter of what happens to us
or is it rather an affair of the heart?

To you, girl, who pin your hopes of happiness on that young man
let me say – he may disappoint you, he must, he's only human,
and you will disappoint him, for you too are only human, and the stars
will often be hidden by clouds, and the thrills will fade
and your heart will be divided between you and me;
there will be happy times, but
this happiness will be at best a word accommodated
to your experience:
the best times only a rumour
of the undivided happiness of heaven.

To you, dancer, who pin your hopes of happiness on strength restored
let me say – it may disappoint you; it must, for you are only human
and will grow old; fashions in entertainment change; only the few
will ever see their name in lights
and your heart will be divided between family and fame;
there will be happy times, but
this happiness will be at best a word accommodated
to your experience:
the best times only a rumour
of the undivided happiness of heaven.

To you, miner, who pin your hopes of happiness on a steady wage
let me say – it may disappoint you, it must, for economics rule:
no job is guaranteed for life, no pension plan assured,
boredom or exhaustion saps that final energy
and your heart will be divided between health and wealth;
there will be happy times, but
this happiness will be at best a word accommodated
to your experience:
the best times only a rumour
of the undivided happiness of heaven.

To you, father, who pin your hopes of happiness on freedom
let me say – it may disappoint you, it must, for freedom is simply space
not only to choose well, but to make more mistakes
and for their consequences to spread further –
and your heart will be divided between right and wrong;
there will be happy times, but

this happiness will be at best a word accommodated
to your experience:
the best times only a rumour
of the undivided happiness of heaven,

for happiness is an affair of the heart
and only the undivided heart
can be wholly happy.

So break my heart, Lord
break it along that line that divides it
into parts ill at ease with themselves and each other:

the part that says 'I need' meaning 'I want'
the part that says 'I can't' meaning 'I can't be bothered'
the part that says 'I gave' meaning 'I invested in the hope
of getting some Brownie points'
the part that says 'I don't love her any more' meaning 'I've found a
better option'
the part that says 'I love you, Lord' meaning 'I need an insurance
policy / company / acceptance'.

Let me see my heart's brokenness, its deceitfulness,
the hopelessness of my journey to wholeness
to the whole happiness of heaven,
unless it is made new.

Break my heart, Lord,
gently so that I don't despair
but firmly, so that I know there's no hope
of trying to piece it together again.

Break my heart, Lord,
for I cannot trust it; break my heart,
for it tempts me with the promise
of the good which masks the best.

So help me to know myself
poor in spirit,
hungry for true goodness,

mourning the world's attempts to market the imitation
as the real thing,
for this is the truth of the matter,
the matter of my heart:
that only now as I hold this hollow thing out to you –
a poor offering, but all for you –
only now can I begin to know my whole heart beat
in time with yours
and begin to sense the stirrings of new life
as your blood transfuses my body,
as I stand rooted by that river that never runs dry
and begin to find fruit in all seasons –
oh, yes Lord!

Yes, Lord –
I guess I *will* mind
when you break my heart; I am only human, and find it hard
to leave my little happiness

but my heart's desire (be patient, Lord!)
is that my heart's desire
is to have a heart,
an undivided heart,
wholly yours, and blessed
with all the great happiness of heaven.

PROPER 3

Fretwork

Genesis 45:3-11, 15; Psalm 37:1-11, 39, 40

'Do not fret: it leads only to evil . . .'

The baby was fretful –
no real reason,
didn't need winding, or changing, or feeding
but he would keep crying,
repeatedly,
wearing me down:
unsettled.

I *tried* to settle him,
kept telling him
'It's all right, I am here!'
but he was too small
and much too preoccupied
with whatever it was that upset him
to heed me.

For many of us, it seems
that is one of the first things we learn:
to fret.

And so it goes on:
    my school shoes are too sensible,
    my asthma stops me body-boarding,
    if only I hadn't chosen that partner/career,
    I need to lose weight, but don't,
    I can't afford to retire and I swear they're watering down the beer;
life is fretful,
unsettled,

and it all keeps going round in my head
niggling; repeating pattern of thought
keeps coming up in my conversation
niggling; repeating pattern of words
rubbing away,
wearing away my contentment,
wearing away the patience of friends,
wearing away, if that were possible,
even the long-suffering of God –

because fretting is the coward's way out.

If I *really* have a problem – with God,
or myself, or life in general –
why don't I have it out with him?
Have an honest-to-God argument,
for heaven's sake,
don't just *mutter* . . .
Or am I afraid he might have an answer?

Fretting is the coward's way out.

If I have a *real* problem – with God,
or myself, or with life in general –
why don't I face it, head on?
Face the heavier questions,
for heaven's sake,
don't just hide behind trivia . . .
Or am I afraid he might change my perspectives?

He has *tried* to settle me,
keeps telling me,
'It's all right, I am here!'
But I am too proud
and much too preoccupied
with whatever it is that's upset me
to heed him.

It's as if, in every event,
I see only the human agency,

the disappointment, the guilt, the botched job,
the unfinished work, the bad decision:
and I fret
because the world is not as it should be,
I am not as I should be
and there's not a lot I can do about it.

In every event,
I fail to see the sovereignty of God
working in ways that are higher than ours, and which ask
not for my understanding,
but for trust.
The world is, for the moment, as it must be,
I am becoming what I should be
and there *is* something I can do about it:

and that is to *choose*
to remember, not the unsatisfactory behaviour
of Joseph's brothers, driven by envy
to sell him down the river:
but the fact that God was at work in the midst
of their machinations to deliver him
where he needed to be for the next chapter
of the divine story.

Worry,
so it is said, is practical atheism;
and what is fretting,
but the illegitimate child of worry?
The fractious crying
of one who does not know his father
God, his father;
whose crying suggests to the world the evil lie
that God does not see
that God does not care
that God does not know the end from the beginning,
that I know better than he
how the world should be –

Lies, all lies.
Be still; those who wait for the Lord,
wait with patient faith, hush their crying
to listen . . . those who have ears to hear,
and who hope in the Lord –
they, the meek, will inherit the earth,
they will be settled in the redeemed earth,
the Lord drying their tears.

My soul,
do not fret
because you do not understand:
trust God, and do good
because that is the evidence of your trust.
Do not fret
because you are not satisfied:
trust God, and do good
because that is the road to contentment.
Do not fret
because you do not see God at work:
trust him, and do good
because that is the very faith that frees him to work.
Be settled,
my soul, in the sovereignty of your God.

Do not fret, it leads only to evil:
take the fretsaw
and cut it out.

Be settled,
my soul, in the sovereignty of your God.

Lent

SECOND SUNDAY BEFORE LENT

Adam and the Identity Parade

Genesis 2:4b-9, 15-25

In the early days, of course, it was all so new and exciting;
I mean, *brand* new,
the architect had only just signed off the plans,
the engineer had only just installed the lighting,
the gardener had only just laid out the grounds
and handed me the keys,
saying, 'Here you are, the Eden project is all yours:
over to you!'

Still early days, of course, and so much to do
and to enjoy: not enough hours in the day,
the trees to be pruned, the lawns mown
the water features carefully maintained,
the borders mulched and vegetables grown, the waste
composted in bins; and all designed to please
the eye and satisfy the taste. So why do I feel
something's missing?

I have, after all, such company! Every form of life is here.
And how to describe you all? Come, let me see –

You shall be – *ant.*
You are furiously busy, super-organised
articulated columns of speeded-up traffic.
I admire and – to some extent – share your work ethic
yet I am not *ant.*

And you shall be – *goat.*
You are voracious; you give me milk, and a good laugh
with your head butts and your long white beard.
I think I might grow one later: and I, too, enjoy my food
yet I am not *goat.*

And you shall be – *parrot.*
You are one of those who can run in the air,
defying gravity, bright rainbow mimic.
From you I hear the sound of my own voice
yet I am not *parrot.*

And you shall be – *ape.*
You bear a passing resemblance to me, with your deft hands
snatching a banana, chattering away,
yet there can be no thought of a proper conversation
for I am not *ape* – and you are not man.

And so they came, all of them
flooding my brain with images,
stretching my vocabulary, blowing my mind,
shouting 'Look at me! Bet you've never seen
the likes of me before! Who am I? Come on, you, man:
find a word for me!'
(Who can blame me if I called that small green fruit
kiwi, forgetting I'd already given the name to a large, flightless bird . . .)

And so they came, all of them,
that extravagant crowd of creatures
jostling to be near me, pressing close,
offering their sweet milk, soft wool, broad back,
doe eyes, rough tongue, wet nose –
I am surrounded: and yet
am I the first to feel
so totally alone among the crowd?

These are all mine, these creatures,
he told me, the Lord God told me;
mine to use for work, for food, for pleasure.
He has given me a measure of his own authority,
sub-contracted steward of all Eden
and I grow, and find much satisfaction
exercising that permissive power, and I am grateful:
yet although everything in the garden is lovely
it is not – quite – the heaven I thought it would be.

But you know what? He's a wily old bird,
the Lord God: I've always told him everything, so
I told him how I felt. 'Let's sleep on it,' he says.
So I did. But he didn't, oh no.
Seems he always has a plan,
something up his sleeve (like a scalpel)
and I have to say,
this time he really excelled himself.
I slept like a log, and woke to find a slight scar on my chest
and the Lord God looking rather pleased with himself
saying 'Come this way, I have something – no, someone to show you.'

And I went, and I looked
and I saw myself – no, not myself.
Another – yet not other, the same,
only different
and my heart leaped, and everything within me spun
and I wanted to race and dance and pull down the sky,
and shout to the whole wide world '*This is the one!*'
and hold quite still to take in the wonder
of the one I shall name *woman . . .*
And the Lord God saw that his plan had come together
and slipped away, leaving us to get to know each other.

I knew that she
was not to be milked, or fleeced or loaded down
with burdens; here was no pack animal,
provider of food, or pet – no,
here was my complement, my perfect help,
and my brain exploded with the revelation
that *it's not about power*
but love.

Under God, I held all power: monarch of all I survey!
No opposition party, none would say me nay
but it was not enough,
was not even what I wanted most. I see now
power without love is a less than human thing,
a battering ram to break down the door;

it takes the love of two, working together,
a lock and key to ease open the door
to humanity.

And was that what the Lord God himself was about,
I wonder, with his sacramental trees?
That he who holds all power
found it was not enough
was not even what he wanted most; that
power without love is a less than divine thing,
an oppressive regime.
It takes the love of two, working together,
divine and human in creative tension
to realise heaven.

There is so much jockeying for power in the garden now,
east of Eden; so much lust for land.
Can't we understand that
power without love makes us little more than animal keepers
of animals, calling them names
to capture their secret strength?
All power will disappoint, corrupt and betray
unless it is power to love

but even the weakest love makes way
for the powerful grace of the Lord God himself
who scans history, choosing
from its grand identity parade all those
who will realise heaven
in love with him.

SUNDAY BEFORE LENT

The Solarium

Exodus 34:29-35; 2 Corinthians 3:12–4:2

Of course it could be simple jealousy,
that there are those with the time, money and figure
to indulge in acquiring a pre-season tan
and then show it off –
but I prefer to think my boycott
of the solarium
is less unprincipled,
is made of sterner stuff.

I mean, what's wrong with the *sun*?
What does it say about us,
that we shrink our gardens –
and sell artificial flowers;
that we overfish our rivers –
and create trout farms;
that we process all the goodness out of our cornflakes –
then put the vitamins back in for an extra 10p?
Are we into so-called 'continuous improvement'
of God's originals?
Or are we just – spineless:
to want the rose without the thorn,
the fish without the wasted afternoon,
breakfast without the need to chew?

And now,
it seems we want the tan
but without the risk of sunburn;
we want the dark skin
but without the daily scraping at parched soil;
we want the warmth
but without breaking sweat.

In short, we want to tame the sun,
make him serve our fads and vanities:
but find we are masters
of a poor thing indeed.

Not an option, though, for Moses – one of the privileged few –
summoned to stand in the full sunlight of God:
and glow! You could see him coming a mile off –
and find in this untamed expression of divine glory
something not a little unsettling,
a burning of one's own cheeks
owing more to shame than sunshine:
heavenly suntan must be more than skin-deep.

For Moses must tell them
the sunburn holiness of God
is no mere aura, no light show,
no mere tingling, spiritual experience;
but, as God's throne was to rest on cherubim
guarding the Covenant's Ark,
so his holiness is the flower springing
from the ground of the law
of his perfect goodness.

And so his people's conscience burns
with the knowledge of guilt
and Moses, too, veils his face,
knowing that, once away from the presence of God
the glow would fade,
the flower would wilt,
finding even in the priest of Israel
no ground of perfect goodness . . .

so God gives Moses a season ticket,
as it were, to come and top up his tan
and remind his people, yet again,
how to grow that flower of holiness.

But down through the ages
the flowers struggle and fade

in their poor ground, refreshed from time to time
by the blood sprinkled,
only to fail again
at the next moral imperative;

and few, precious few are summoned
to stand in the full sun
and refract its fire to earth . . .

Until the time comes for God to form
his holiness, his burning brightness
into his own Son and be born among us
where we can see, and hear and touch:
and not be consumed in an instant, true –
but don't be deceived . . .
There, on the mountain top, in clouds of glory
Jesus succeeds Elijah and Moses:
'This is my Son: listen to him!'
And he writes his essential law on our hearts,
receives us through the blood of his Son
and seals us with his Holy Spirit,
setting us the joint task
of ploughing up that poor ground
and producing flowers of holiness.

Flowers of holiness
growing in the sunlight of his presence
and the ground of his perfect goodness.

So who needs a solarium?

We live no longer in a land
where sun is scarce and unreliable,
and our exposure to it rationed
to a few protected hours: no!
We can stand on the ground of the perfect goodness of Christ
and reach through the clouds
to the sunlight of God
any day of the year,

any time of the day or night
and glow!

I don't need to pay: thanks to Christ
I have my life membership, and beyond;
I don't need to replace the bulbs in the lamps:
God is the light, and the warmth, and the joy of the world for ever;
I don't need to book an appointment
to come to top up my tan:
I can *live* in the presence of God 24/7 . . .

And as I look at him
and allow him to look at me,
as I whisper a prayer
and see that he has heard,
as I bow in response
to his wise and loving word,
hush my shrillness,
take on stillness,
so he will slowly burn
his image in me;

as I live in the sunlight of his presence
so the Spirit will take the perfect goodness of Christ,
dig it in to my poor ground
deep, more than skin-deep,
work from the inside out
to grow flowers of holiness which will glow,
glow! and never fade:
colour me glorious.

FIRST SUNDAY OF LENT

Angels and Demons

Psalm 91:1, 2, 9-16; Luke 4:1-13

That's the best part of a good spy story:
that we don't know who's on which side.
Who can we trust?
Not till the last page
do we know who has lied,
whether the good or the bad have died . . .

Fiction's one thing – fact's another:
not knowing who's on which side,
who you can trust,
is the worst part
of a messy affair like Iraq
or a terrorist suicide.

Trust me!
I'm a doctor
lawyer priest insurance salesman.
Trust me!
I'm a banker
politician cabby journalist.
Trust me!
I'm your father
sister best mate counsellor.
Trust me!
I'm your guru
spiritual director god.

How am I to know who to believe
when everyone has their price
and the devil quotes Scripture?

We have prided ourselves
on asking so many questions,
voicing so many doubts,
challenging every 'truth',
leaving open every door:
it seems we have left ourselves
very little ground to stand on
and clutch now at any straw,
to keep from falling
into a sea of uncertainty.

As the man said,
he who stands for nothing
will fall for anything.

Did God say . . . ?
and can we believe him?
Let's take a straw poll:

Adam and Eve: Well, yes, God said . . .
but no, we don't feel like believing him –
and look what happened to them.
And us.

Moses: Yes, God said . . .
and yes, Israel, you'd better believe it –
but they didn't and life, far from being a beach,
was a desert.

The psalmist: Yes, God said . . .
and yes, I believe
his angels will guard me; I trust, and enjoy
his top security.

Jesus: Yes, God said . . .
and I don't for a minute doubt
that I am his Son and can trust him in life and in death:
get behind me, Satan!

The devil: Yes, God said . . .
and yes, I believe it (and tremble) –
but I'm damned if I'm going to accept it, and neither are you,
if I have my way . . .

And how things have changed – For now
most of us haven't a clue if God said
anything at all, let alone whether we believe it;
which god are we talking about, anyway,
and what is truth? Only what's true for me . . .
And as for trust – well, you can't be too careful these days:
or can you?
We speak of a sea of faith,
and spiritual voyages of discovery:
I wonder, though, if the sea
on which we are tossed by every wave of doctrine
isn't a sea of doubt which, for some reason,
we seem to prefer
to the solid rock of God.

Has he had his way,
the one who wears not horns and a forked tail
but a very reasonable, caring face,
sometimes even a clerical collar?

The one who dresses demons like angels
and sends them, spiritualised
or trivialised
into the world to rob and confuse us?

The one who persuades us, 'Don't eat the onion,
be nourished and grow: but rip it off!
layer by layer, and find there is nothing left
but hunger'?

He's certainly done a good job, taking
a proper need to make use of our God-given brains
and turning it into an arrogance
which fixes doubt as the bottom line:

you, God, along with that guy in the dirty raincoat,
indeed, along with all forms of authority
are guilty – or at least suspect –
until we prove your innocence.

Do we then suppose God to be a liar?
Oh! How much we have lost,
when we cannot say,
'Though everyone *else* be a liar,
let God be proved true!'
Jesus overcame evil
through his unshakeable trust
in his loving, heavenly Father.
So can we.

That's the best part of our story:
that there *is* one we can trust
absolutely;
but the proving is in the trusting:
not till the last page
will the reader know
that we were right,
absolutely,
to take him at his word.

SECOND SUNDAY OF LENT

Like There's No Tomorrow

Genesis 15:1-12, 17, 18; Psalm 27; Philippians 3:17–4:1; Luke 13:31-35

And he said to them,
'Do not be like the man in the sleeper compartment
who unpacked his suitcase,
spread all his things around
and made himself at home,
saying, "This is a reasonably pleasant place,
food adequate, facilities not too bad:
would prefer an en suite, but never mind."
And so he lived from day to day,
eating, sleeping, and generally amusing himself,
happy, or unhappy enough –

'but never, once, did he pull up the blind,
look out of the window, and realise
that the background noise
and the gentle jolting
spelt T – R – A – I – N;
that he was *travelling,*
and that one day, soon, he would reach
a destination.

'No, do not be like that man.

'Rather, get out your ticket,
see the name of your destination,
read the literature provided,
unpack only your overnight bag
and be ready:
like it or not, you are *travelling*
and one day, soon, you will arrive –

'so be ready to get off,
step out into daylight
into your destiny,
your promised destination.

Live today in the light of tomorrow.'

But today we live like there's no tomorrow

like the credit will never be called in
like earth's resources will go on for ever
like it's all too complex to understand anyway,
so what the hell? Live for the moment: tomorrow may never come.

Oh, but it will! God promised.
It's on the ticket,
the ticket God issued to Abraham
four thousand years ago, stamped
with that gracious promise,
that through his descendants
all the nations of the world will be blessed;
God gave him his ticket
and sent him travelling, and Abraham
lived his today in the light of that tomorrow
which he would never see
but which would come;
and so he was counted
faithful,
righteous,
friend of God.

But today we live like there's no tomorrow.

Carpe diem! We press the words into our service:
seize the moment
the bargain the new drug
the woman the trip the special loan:
try it today! Why resist temptation
when we can give in? Why delay?

Now is the time to top up our experience;
now is the day of instant gratification,
never mind what it does
to our stress levels,
our solvency,
our soul.

We give our minds to earthly things
which fill not only our mental space
but our time, our conversation, the places
we call home: and finally
we invite all those possessions to fill our hearts
to possess us,
to define us,
until we forget (if we ever knew)
that we don't belong here:
we are citizens not of earth but of heaven
and all these things
are God's provision on our journey
to leave them behind.

Live today in the light of tomorrow:
heaven glimpsed in the promise of God
is worth weeping for, wanting for,
waiting for.

To live today as if there were no tomorrow
at the time may seem like fun;
I can eat, drink and make merry,
borrow from Peter to pay Paul
hush any hint of disquiet.

But one day
I will see my life today
in the light of God's tomorrow
and I will need to explain,
explain why I did not look out of the window
to see the world rushing past
as I sped from the present into the future;

explain why I did not read my ticket,
believe in my destiny, my destination,
trust in the promise of God;
explain why I did not speak to the people
waiting at each suburban station
and help them onto the train;
one day,
when borrowed time must be accounted for
in God's eternity.

The promise of God
renders tomorrow more real than today;

to live like there's no tomorrow
is but the fool's attempt
to duck responsibility,
to trick despair;
unaware
that, standing on the promises of God,
he can reach hope,
the certain hope of arriving home
on time,
God's appointed time:
if not today,
tomorrow.

THIRD SUNDAY OF LENT

Hurry Now, While Stocks Last

Isaiah 55:1-9; Luke 13:1-9

Open the newspaper,
and out flutters half a forest of flyers –
amazing, not-to-be-missed offers on this, and that
and mainly the other:
loose covers, decking, deep fat fryers
and blinds, always Venetian blinds;
does anyone actually use Venetian blinds these days
(or is it just a warehouse in Walsall,
repository for the world's last remaining slatted wonders?).

We are such suckers for a bargain,
(we in the affluent West),
stopping off at the hole in the wall
on our way to rummage through the charity shops
(just after Christmas is best);
my brother claims that all
his CDs come from the £5 rack in HMV.
Yes, I say,
but you don't *like* Shostakovich.

So why do we,
self-styled experts in spotting a good offer at a hundred paces
consistently miss
the best offer of all?

'Come, all you who are thirsty,
come, buy wine and milk
without money and without cost.'

Are we not thirsty, then?
Despite the vast array of labels at the bar

and four whole aisles at Asda
I would dare to say
that we are.

Blessed with the world's goods, or deprived,
all alike
thirst
to know the meaning of the journey,
to know love as our travelling companion,
to know we have arrived,
finally, at its intended end.
And all alike
are weary,
weary of walking the same way
weary of falling short,
weary of the weight of doubt
and of hanging in there.

Thirsty, yes: a soul thirst;
but looking to God?
No way! Rather die first . . .
Coca-cola, after all,
is the real thing.
Weary, yes: and worn down;
but coming to Christ?
No way! We'd rather drown
our sorrows, and ring
our therapist.

Because, I guess, a bargain is one thing; a free gift is quite another.

Paying *something* discharges our obligations.

And in any case, we all know there's no such thing as a free lunch.

We know the free gift will be a small plastic letter opener,
and that they're bribing us to take their catalogue.
And we know they know we know
but we all play the game of contract dog-eat-dog,

except for God, who clearly
plays by quite different rules.

Having thoughts that are not our thoughts,
ways that are not our ways,
he gives us no chance
to pride ourselves on having snapped up a bargain; rather
he gives us the chance
to humble ourselves in accepting the truly free gift
that cost our Father dearly.

Is there, then, a price to be paid after all?
Only in what it will cost us to come,
only in what that coming will cost us to leave behind:
pride

and complacency?
Can we afford to delay?
Why does the prophet say
'Seek the Lord while he may be found,
call on him while he is near'?
And why does Jesus speak of the fig tree's last chance?

Hurry now, while stocks last!

But surely there is no expiry date
on the offer of salvation?
Surely the grace of God
can never be in short supply?

No, never.
But while it is true that the invitation
is to *all* who are thirsty
to *anyone* who believes,
that it *always* has my name on, and yours
and no one need ever be left outside –
yet there *will* come a day,
that day when the guest list is closed,
when it will be too late to *répondez s'il vous plaît;*

when the music stops, and you have to freeze,
just as you are,
wishing you hadn't been caught on one foot
with your mouth open and your shirt hanging out,
but it's too late;
and of course that day
could be today.
I have no way of knowing how long
my stock of time will last.

Just as the fig tree was bare,
the Jews refusing the water of life
that would ripen the fruit to feed the world,
so we can refuse the milk and the wine
condemning ourselves to become
those who crave only that which will lead to death.

At the end of the day,
no one will be force-fed
and the life support machine will be turned off.

Is God, then, a high-pressure salesman,
always looking to close with the offer?
Is he, then, the great evangelist,
getting us up out of our seats to decide for him?

Pressure, no;
urgency, yes – and such love;
to our God belong mercy and forgiveness
and the words of eternal life.
The most precious possessions in all the world
are his to give
and ours to receive.
Come, now –
why wait?

FOURTH SUNDAY OF LENT (MOTHERING SUNDAY)

Shoes

Luke 15:1-3, 11b-32

What is a Christian?
Someone who has been forgiven
everything
thanks
to Jesus;

a wanderer returned,
a slave set free,
a starving man come into a land of plenty;
a dying man become a new creation:
it's all there,
in the story of the prodigal
love of the father
for his wayward son,

in the story of the prodigal
love of God the Father
for all of us wayward sons and daughters.

Wayward? What, us? All of us?
Yes, all of us.
Which of us has never gone his own way – and known himself lost,
voiced his own thoughts – and wished he had bitten his tongue,
let his mind wander – and blushed,
ignored his God – and discovered it does not work
to pretend those warning signs
are merely age, or stress or bad legislation,
vestiges of an old-fashioned morality,
bad luck or indigestion?

No, it does not work:
those signs are there for a reason,

so let's beware of thanking God
that we are not like this prodigal son!
If we had his lottery win, his inheritance,
his chances and temptations,
who's to say we'd not end up among the pigs?
It's only a matter of degree
and God judges not by degrees
but by principle

and with what grace!

From a million miles away, he knows
that instant his son faces up to himself,
when the tears of self-pity
become that sorrow of soul
that yearns for a new beginning. Yes,
the father knows
and goes at once for the robe and the ring
and the shoes – yes, the shoes . . .

The robe that speaks not just
of material exchange
of sweat-stained scraps for freshly laundered shirt
but of spiritual exchange:
the filthy rags of our worst failures and also our best attempts
for Christ's robe of pure righteousness . . .

The ring that speaks not just
of belonging again, of welcome back
into the family heart and home
but of spiritual welcome:
engagement ring for the church, the bride to be
of Christ, heaven's eager groom . . .

And the shoes – yes, the shoes that speak not just
of comfort and relief
for bruised and dirty feet
but also of social and political relief:
bare feet being a mark of slavery,
whilst free men were shod . . .

Also of spiritual relief:
priests of old, slaves still to sin,
went barefoot in the presence of God
whilst we, thanks to the ransom paid by Christ,
are slaves set free,
brought into the family of God,
walking tall, wearing shoes,
the shoes of the gospel of peace.

I am convicted by these shoes!
Convicted of my bad attitude to shoes,
of my grudging acceptance of such necessary evils –
necessary to shield my too soft flesh
from fresh gravel and frostbite;
evil because they are single-handedly
(or double-footedly?) responsible
for most of the dirt on my freshly cleaned carpet.
Why doesn't anyone ever remember
to take them off and leave them in the hall?
And if they're a nice colour, you can never get polish to match
and the comfortable ones look like nothing on earth
and the elegant ones hurt like hell
and they smell.

Forgive me, Lord;
from now on, may I look at shoes in a different light:
as a focus for faith.
As I tighten a buckle or fasten a lace
remind me that, thanks to your gift of grace,
I am no more a slave; I am free! Free
to walk away from all that would tempt me to stray; free
from regret and the guilt of the past; free
to stand in the presence of God; free
to explore where I've never dared before; free
to dance with joy that I am forgiven,
forgiven, and on my way! Free!

but committed to choose,
now, the shoes of the gospel,

the shoes of the gospel of peace,
peace with God my maker, judge – and father.
Free to run and tell a barefoot, orphan race
that they, too, have a father:
Father who seeks his sons with a prodigal love,
longing to give them the shoes
made especially for them
when they were no more than a twinkle in his eye.

From now on, I *will* look at shoes in a different light,
let them remind me, as I put them on,
that I am one who is free, forgiven
everything
thanks
to Jesus.

Let them remind me, as I take them off,
that I am one who is bound by love
to Jesus
whose service
is perfect freedom.

FIFTH SUNDAY OF LENT

Down Is the New Up

Psalm 126; Philippians 3:4b-14

No, this is not a plea for pessimism
nor a permission for wet blankets
of all ages or persuasions
to wag the finger knowingly and say,
'Too good to be true!
Never rains but it pours!
All good things come to an end!
No one's luck can last for ever . . .'

No, it is simply to recognise
that in the lives of everyone I know about
(everyone, that is, who's honest)
there is a mix of ups and downs,
joys and sorrows,
pains and pleasures,
tears and laughter:
the tide comes in – and it goes out.

Good news!
God delivers his people from Egypt,
wipes out the opposition with a single blow –
now, surely, the Israelites are on a roll –
But the not-so-good news
is that there are still many battles to be fought,
many deaths died
if the Jews are to possess the promised land.

Good news!
God delivers his people from exile,
leads them back to Jerusalem –
now, surely, there are good times ahead –

But the not-so-good news
is long, dangerous months of travelling
only to find that 'home' lies in ruins:
Utopia is yet to be built.

So yes! We remember
that God has worked miracles,
truly, done great things for us
and we are glad.
We remember too, though,
that it didn't last:
there were always new enemies,
and the streams in the desert dried up.

Are we not ready, then,
to walk in the freedom won for us,
to take the olive branch offered to us,
to hold the blessing?
Must we always slip back,
binding ourselves to the world's ways,
falling out with our fellow men,
finding no road is ever straight?

Even the most committed Christian,
the greatest saint –
perhaps especially these,
good men whose steps are ordered by the Lord –
may find those steps take them by strange ways,
through dark and painful days:
no guarantees, then,
that obedience brings ease.

But when we take a pen,
and chart our life's course:
mountains and valleys,
high points and low –
and now, a second line:
when were we most aware
of the presence of God?
When did we *grow?*

Is it coincidence,
that the times when we were bowed down
with greater trials and testing
were also those times when we cried aloud
to God, stretching our faith, it seemed,
to breaking point
yet proving him greater still –
and so we grew?

From his grace, God gives a taste
of blessing, stirs our soul's hunger for him.
That *state* of blessedness,
must wait, though –
must wait on heaven,
must wait on holiness
holiness won through obedience
in the darkness.

Even Christ learns obedience
through suffering;
he who raised Lazarus from the dead,
with anointed feet
walks straight to his own death, knowing
that faith must reach the finishing line
and how often the way up
is down.

And we, who glibly say 'Oh yes,
we would be more Christ-like!'
must then become like him
in accepting death:
death to our claims of capability
death to our own aims and agenda,
admitting that here is something we can't handle
but Christ-in-us can – and to *him* be the glory!

So much, then, for our mantra
of *continuous improvement,*
our massaging of statistics
to prove it;

God does not chart success
by our seven rules:
down is the new up
when it comes to holiness.

One day, no mere stream
but the river of life itself
will flow through the desert, and
Christmas roses will bloom all year round;
till then, remind us, Lord
that you bring water from solid rock
and glaze your temples
from grains of sand.

PALM SUNDAY

For Crying Out Loud

Luke 19:28-40; Philippians 2:5-11

Do you know
that if you are lucky, if you are very alert,
and still,
you can see, just for a sliver of time
through a tiny tear in the fabric that muffles the world
to the joy beneath?

One of those days
in late spring, when the beech trees take me by surprise,
again,
with their impossibly luminous green
and I am captivated, not by a beautiful tree, but by
the genius of *green*

or listening
as the music hits the frequency of the earth itself
and *sings*
and every solid object and objection shatters
leaving only the absolute certainty
of harmony,

or joining the crowd
on its way to Jerusalem, knowing that here,
at last,
is the promised King, and *all will be well*
and, as I pause for breath, hearing the very stones
cry out for joy.

But the seam of joy
runs deep, so often barely detected, or suspected:
bedrock

beneath the patchwork of good and bad and mediocre
and those who would mine it must be prepared
to suffer.

The greening
comes only after the death of winter
leaves bare;
the musical climax only after an orgy of discord,
frustration, near misses, and years
of practice;

the rapturous welcome
for Jesus the King of kings soon, so soon to be
cut short
as the road to freedom takes a sudden U-turn
to Golgotha, and the blank, black incomprehension
of the cross.

What, then, is the stuff of joy
and what its justification?

Joy is Jesus
sent, not as the King in the fairy tale charges
the prince,
'I have a somewhat unpleasant task for you:
a small matter of slaying a dragon or two, in order to win
the princess' –

Jesus sent,
or rather, not sent but choosing of his own free will to
resign
his divine entitlement and undergo the most absolute
incredible, mind-blowing metamorphosis
of all time;

becoming for us
God without glory or knowledge or power
except
what his Father showed him: in order to show us

every detail of God that can be kept, expressed
in human form.

And this is joy,
surely, to know that we are understood
by him,
the one who matters most to us; known
because *his* heart beat with human flesh and blood
and he wept;

known by him
in the way that the lightest touch of a hand,
a word,
the swiftest meeting of eyes is enough, and more than enough
between lovers or friends, to say what cannot be said,
to say it all;

and I can let go
and allow myself to rest in the knowledge that
he knows,
he understands me better than I understand myself
yet wisely chooses that he will never
invade my space.

And this is joy,
surely, that Jesus gave what no other lamb could give:
consent
to be sacrificed, to lay down that life
that none could take from him, knocking death out
for the count of three,

setting us free
from the treadmill, the cause and effect of sin
and death,
reassured, as we triumph or trip in our own
daily skirmishes, that the final word is with God: the final
battle is won.

And this, too, is joy,
surely, that Jesus is back where he belongs,

restored
to the place of glory at the right hand of God;
he who humbles himself shall be exalted,
even our Lord.

This is our joy,
that the no-man's land between God and creation
is crossed,
the blackest hole in the universe filled
with the love of God, and at the name of Jesus
every knee shall bow!

Were it not so,
were this not our God, our God of amazing love
and grace,
I wonder if we would ever glimpse joy
in pure colour, or sound – ever be stopped in our tracks
by ecstasy;

but this, this is the stuff of joy;
this is its justification.

Watch, then
for you never know when joy will surprise you;
treasure
those times: they are no mere fancy, but the universe crying out loud
that the bottom line is the immeasurable, unutterable, hilarious
love of God.

Easter

EASTER DAY

Giving God a Decent Burial

John 20:1-18

'Don't talk to me about God,' said the old lady;
'I've spent fifty years looking
for some sign that it's all true,
and what have I found?
Not a thing.
I'm much happier now that I've decided
I'm an atheist.'

Looking for God and not finding him,
leading to denial
or, perhaps more often, to doubt;
needles in haystacks
are child's play
compared with searching the universe for –
for we're not sure quite what . . .

Looking for God and not finding him,
not always leading to doubt
or denial, though; curiously enough,
it can prompt belief.
Look at John, on that first Easter morning:
finding no one
he found faith.

The empty tomb
stands at the crossroads of doubt and belief,
invites me first to come and bury
all *my* gods,
seal them in with that large stone
and without tears,
inscribe their names:

Here lies the body of god, my god
who would not have allowed my rabbit, my granddad, my baby
to die, despite my prayer;
the body of god
who, I thought, had my happiness
as his prime concern:
this, *my* god, isn't there.
So, bury this idol fancy
and look elsewhere.

Here lies the body of god, my god
who would never have watched, aloof,
as the earth quaked
and the tide rose, the roof fell in
and the homeless froze,
blood caked in open wounds;
the body of god
who, I thought, should preside
over a world of peace and plenty:
this, *my* god, isn't there.
So, bury this idol fancy
and look elsewhere.

Here lies the body of god, my god
who seems to incite his fans to murderous frenzy
cruel crusading,
mad martyrdom –
or to nothing more than
non-committal niceness,
cucumber sandwich Christians
who sit kindly enough over tea
but stand for nothing;
the body of god
who, I thought, is to blame
for all, or nothing:
this, *my* god, isn't there.
So, bury this idol fancy
and look elsewhere.

The trouble with God is that, like my umbrella,
he has this habit of not being found
where you last left him.

That's what comes of not being dead –
(sorry, Nietzsche)
you can trust a dead body to stay put –
but to live means change,
movement, being about one's business
of creating new heavens and a new earth.

So heaven knows
where you might find him:
'Look! He's behind you!
No, it's not the gardener, Mary,
it's God, on his way to an important meeting
so don't detain him now.'

It is always hard to hold on
to a favourite form of God –
he wills it so.
Though he will not move on
without leaving a sign,
grave clothes neatly folded, marking a stage,
and a calling by name:

'I am yours, Mary, and you are mine:
no one can steal you away from me,
nor me from you;

'I am, and am not, what you thought:
I do deal in happiness, but know
it is not to be found on the surface of things;
I do heal some of the suffering now, but show
hands scarred in the bringing of longer-term aid;
I do field all kinds of blame, but sow
seeds of forgiveness where guilt is owned.

'I am Jesus bar Joseph
but I am also Emmanuel.

I am thirty-three
but I am older than the world.
I am undoubtedly human
but no less certainly divine.
I have walked the earth which I created,
talked with the men formed in my image;
lived, and died as a man, I who will judge all men . . .

'You think you know me
but I am, and am not, what you thought –

and I am certainly not dead.

'Listen! Do you hear me call you by name?
Or do you just hear words,
words with sense but no significance?
Listen, listen! Hear your name
and know my voice;
do not despair
when you do not find me;
the god you cannot find is not worth looking for;
a dead loss
deserving only a decent burial.

'Keep looking;
keep listening,
keep daring to believe that I am greater,
deeper, not absent but present in a different way,
tying up the ends of time,
dying only to be on my way
and to take you with me,

Mary?'

SECOND SUNDAY OF EASTER

Eyewitness

Acts 5:27-32; Revelation 1:4-8; John 20:19-31

It wasn't as scary as I thought,
going to the police station;
they asked me what I'd seen,
asked me to put my name to it
and that was that.
Being a witness has to be much easier
than being judge or jury,
having to understand each explanation,
to sift, to weigh, to be responsible
for the outcome.

See – and tell:
that's all there is to it.

Jesus saw what his Father was doing:
how on earth? By sight,
or insight or revelation
from the Spirit? Never mind how. He saw,
and told the world.
He was 'the faithful witness':
not judge or jury,
coming with condemnation
but simply, obediently
offering hope.

See – and tell:
that's all there is to it.

Thomas – I think he was blinded
by grief and desolation,
unable to see with the eye of faith

or trust the witness of friends
until Jesus,
knowing his heart, appeared
and spoke to his desperation
and Thomas *saw*, and could not help but speak
of what he had seen, that Christ is
both Lord and God.

See – and tell:
that's all there is to it.

Peter and the other apostles
who caused consternation,
setting the whole of Jerusalem talking
with what they had seen of the witness
of Christ on earth;
setting the whole Sanhedrin fuming
with what they now saw of the role
of Christ in bringing salvation,
the greatest news story that ever broke
and must be told.

See – and tell:
that's all there is to it.

See – and tell: that's all very well,
you may say: they happened to be
in the right place, at the right time.
When the rumours of incarnation reached them, they
could go and *see*;
but what about *me?*
I have only been able to listen to friends,
to read from a book, to follow the church,
to hope for the best: what if I *don't* see –
only believe?

See – and tell:
how can *I* do it?

Hold on a minute – the things of God
are only ever discerned with the eye of faith;
most of those who witnessed the coming of Christ on earth
followed a miracle-man: but quickly deserted a
crucified God;
the chief priests refused even to speak his name;
the religious right plotted his downfall;
the people, as ever, were fickle almost to a man – no,
they did not *see* then, any more
than we do now.

See – and tell:
they didn't do it.

Be thankful for doubting Thomas,
the one for whom seeing was believing,
for giving Jesus the chance to put him straight:
'Blessed are those who *don't* see
and yet believe!'
If it were all as plain as the nose on your face
where would be the risk, the trust,
the adventure, the merit, the love – the worth
of knowing God? Blessed are those
whose ground is faith . . .

Believe – and tell
what you see with the eye of faith.

Faith is choosing to hold
that God is good; faith is choosing to 'see'
the hand of God in creation, the purpose of God
being worked out through good times and bad,
God in control;
faith is saying *I will*
I will 'see' the hand of God in my life,
not 'luck' be it good or bad, not fate or coincidence
but the love of the God in whom I live, and move and
have my being.

Believe – and tell:
that's all there is to it.

Without faith it's impossible
for us to please God: it is, after all,
the highest response of which we human creatures
are capable, since we could never bear the *sight* of God
in all his glory,
which alone would convince the world. But one day –
this is our faith – one day we *shall see* him come
with clouds of glory; then every eye *shall* see him, every knee bow
and every tongue tell the angels,
'Jesus is Lord of all!'

See – and tell:
but for some, too late . . .

Summon our faith, then –
not a feeling, but *willing* to choose
in favour of God, *willing* to put our mouth
where our money is, *willing* to lose our life, and
find it in him;
not only does that willingness start to grow
a stronger faith, but we begin to catch rumours of heaven,
begin to glimpse the edges of glory,
begin to speak with growing conviction, that
all this is true.

Believe – and tell:
this is the way to see.

THIRD SUNDAY OF EASTER

Damascus Road Signs

Acts 9:1-20

Journeys are good,
good for reflecting,
physical and geographical reflecting,
spiritual and emotional,
anticipating, open
to be surprised by new horizons –

Jerusalem to Jericho road
reflecting on what we know
of neighbourliness:
on what we really know
when our time, or our pocket, or our weakness is touched,
when our neighbour is the Samaritan we despise . . .

Emmaus road,
brief encounter that opened eyes,
kindled hope, sparked faith:
entertaining
no mere angel but God himself
unawares.

And of course Damascus road,
birthplace of that
'Damascus road experience'
much mocked or coveted:
reason for faith
and for lack of faith.

I guess the Highway Code
took on a whole new meaning that day
when God showed Saul
his way:

Warning lightning flash!
No mere power cable overhead
but the lightning of Christ himself, enthroned,
shooting from heaven,
glory of God, whose radiance
Saul had glimpsed before in the face of Stephen stoned
while he approved,
glory of God, whose radiance
no man can look on and live
leaving Saul as if dead.

Warning exclamation!
No mere pothole or cattle crossing
but the voice of Christ himself, exalted,
shouting from heaven
'Listen! Listen to me, your God!
I am Jesus, whom you are hunting down . . .'
And in that 'I am', the realisation
that halted Saul in his tracks:
if Christ be not dead
but alive
then Christ must be – could he be – *God?*

No through road!
No mere signing of cul de sac or byway
but the warning of Christ himself, Alpha and Omega,
who sees the end from the beginning,
disclosing from heaven
that the end of the road
for the angry, the proud
the coldly self-righteous – and more,
for the nice, the well-meaning, the 'good',
for all who can sing with Sinatra 'I did it my way' –
that the end of that way,
is the end of the way of sinning:
if the wages of sin is death
then the end of that road
is a dead end.

Give way!
No mere alert to lorries reversing
but the plea of Christ himself, the Lamb once slain to make that bridge
to God, cancelling our sin, suffering our pain,
imploring from heaven
our willingness
to cede right of way to him whose right it is:
to concede that Jesus, redeemer, saviour and friend,
the truth, the life, the way
should have the final say.

Blind person crossing!
I bet that sign wasn't there yesterday.

And the one that is only in God's Highway Code
not 'No U-turn'
but yes, please, right here and now
U-turn:
you
turn.

Well, it's all very well for Saul.
I mean – a conversion like that!
It wasn't like that at all
for me or my friends at church –
at least, not as far as I know;
we don't discuss these things much.

For Saul
the all-singing, all-dancing version,
glorious technicolour, Dolby sound,
supernatural disco,
(strobes OTT, though, could sue them for that).
Could hardly miss it:
God reached down . . .

For me,
I confess that I found it all rather ordinary,
muted tones that might

or might not have been God:
a friend admired, a scripture shedding light,
a habit of prayer –
did God reach down, or am I still
stretching up?

For Saul
it was all or nothing.
He was that sort of guy:
if a thing's worth doing, then all your heart
and all your mind, and all your soul, and all your strength,
110 per cent is barely enough;
no doubt, distraction or deflection,
all out.

For me,
always a question,
gaps for the winds of the world to whistle through,
whipping my thoughts into tangles
and my will to wool;
unsure about whom I address
when I pray 'Lord, I believe: please help my unbelief'.

For Saul,
unexpected, out of the blue,
out of a clear blue sky
interrupting a firm purpose,
undermining a clear mission;
God's action
dramatic (but on prepared ground,
the foundation stones falling around
the first martyr).

For me,
line upon line, precept upon precept,
thinking it through,
reasoning as far as reasoning goes;
eternity on my mind
but nobody knows
the beginning nor the end of it.

For Saul
a revolution,
chalk and cheese,
utter transformation;
there on his knees he receives his sight
through one who can call him 'brother'
and the Spirit of God turns his life around,
astounding
confounding expectation.

For me,
small step by step –
two forward, one back;
change, if at all, is far too slow
or am I not as willing as I claim?
Some changes spell pain.
Lord, make me worthy of the name I profess.

So – can this be the same
experience, Saul's and mine?
Which road is right, Damascus
or my suburban avenue?
Conversion . . . what's the bottom line?
I used to learn that all roads lead to Rome.
Which road is right?

All that start with that U-turn
and follow – not the way, the road
to Christ, but the way
which *is* Christ.

FOURTH SUNDAY OF EASTER

Rags: A Parable

Revelation 7:9-17

'When I was a kid, we used to do this all the time.'
Sas takes a couple of steps up the escalator
and leans on the handrail.

'What, shopping?'

'Nah, going up and down the escalators in all the big stores.
All the way up and all the way down. Never bought anything.
Just looking . . .'

'Bit like now,' says Dilly.

Flints is one of those annoying stores
where you have to walk right round to find the next UP escalator:
but all the way up, they don't pause to look at anything.
Single-minded, they head for the top floor; they have their system.

The top floor is smart blue-rinse classics and power dressing for business wannabes. Sas and Dilly try to look nonchalant and rely on the 'customer first' training which will stop staff cold-shouldering them or suggesting they're on the wrong floor.

'Sas, look at this!'
A row of smart grey tweedy suits,
displayed with cream silk blouses and a golden rose in the lapel.
'Why would anyone wear *that?* It's uniform – like St Mag's posh school.'

'Won't get onto the fête committee without it.
Need to change the rose, though. Not so exclusive
if they all turn up with the same one.'
She rummages for the price tag. 'Eighty quid!! And that's just the jacket!'

'I'm going to try one of these – just for a laugh.'
Dilly picks up a navy jacket with impressive shoulder padding.
She slips out of her fleece and struggles with the buttons.
'Nah, not very comfortable.' She turns to Sas.
'Do these things really get you a job?'

'Not if you wear them with jeans and trainers.'

'Nah, seriously. They're supposed to make you look like you know what you're doing, like you're the boss and everyone had better take notice.'
She draws herself up and looks over pretend specs at Sas.
'Come into my office at once, Miss Webber . . .'

'Do you need any help?'
The assistant's jacket also has shoulder padding.

'Er – no thanks; don't think it's really me.'
Dilly hastily hands back the jacket and fetches her fleece.
'Come on Sas, let's go down.' They make for the escalator.

'Here, this is new!' Sas pulls Dilly past the coats and rainwear.
'This boutiquey place, with all the ethnic stuff.'

'I quite fancy it,' says Dilly. 'It's like it says you're going to be different, be comfortable, wear what you like, never mind what's in fashion.
Colours run, though.'

'My cousin's into all that,' Sas says. 'Hangs out with the hippy crowd.
They're a bit weird. That's the trouble; you look like that
and everyone thinks you're veggie and ride a clapped-out bike
and never potty train your kids cos they don't wear anything anyhow.'

'Don't be daft.' Dilly rummages along the rack.
'I like the free spirit bit, but I don't do fringes.'

Round the corner is sportswear.
'Don't know why they bother,' says Dilly,
'what with the High Street shops always having closing down sales.'

'Did you see Stevie's got all this amazing Speedex gear,
and he's never been near a sports pitch in his life?'

'I reckon it's tough for a bloke, though, not being into sport.
I can understand him wanting to get in with the rest of the crowd.'

'It's a fraud.' Sas isn't convinced. 'Pretending to be something you're not.'

'I like the rugby shirts. They cost a bomb, though.'

'And you don't play rugby. Come on, ground floor's best.'

Flints aren't daft.
Impulse buys between the escalator and the doors.
Here are the trendy, new season disposables.

'*Who* decides the colours?' asks Sas. 'The blue's OK, but that pink's cringeable. Even my kid sister wouldn't wear it.'

'I need some new jeans,' says Dilly.
'All mine are bootleg; they should be really skinny now.'

'Ooh, I like this T-shirt; I think I'll get one.'

'Your mum won't like the off-the-shoulder!'

'Don't care if mum likes it or not: Matt will!' Sas takes three tops, a pair of jeans and a sweater into the fitting room. They both squeeze in and draw the curtain. Fifteen minutes later, Sas buys the blue top and Dilly buys the jeans (tomorrow she'll come back and change them for the ones with diamanté).

They make their way down the High Street,
taking a quick inventory of their contemporaries who, of course,
are doing exactly the same.
Sas giggles and points. Dilly nods agreement.

'Ooh, look – aren't they sweet?' They pause outside Gap Kids.

'I'm not sure about really little kids' fashion,' says Dilly.
'I mean, little kids ought to wear old stuff and have fun and get dirty, didn't they?'

'It's for the mums really,' says Sas.
'So the other mums will be impressed and think the kids are great because they look great. Look, that one's even got a little sheepskin coat and climbing socks!'

'Come on, we'll miss the bus.'

The bus drops them half a mile from the village;
they walk slowly down the lane, swinging their Flints bags.

'Hey, stop a minute!' Dilly climbs the farm gate. 'Look at the lambs – black ones too.'

'Do you know what my dad told me?' Sas joins her.
'Sometimes the ewe dies while she's having the lamb;
and quite often, if a ewe has twins, one of them dies –
so the ewe that's lost one lamb will look after the orphan.'

'That's cool.'

'Yeah, but what they have to do is, they skin the dead lamb
and put the lambskin on the orphan lamb, so the ewe will accept it
because it looks and smells like it belongs to her.'

'Ugh, that's gross!' Dilly looks horrified. 'But I suppose if it means it's accepted . . .'

'Come on,' says Sas, pulling her off the gate.
'I must wash my hair before Matt gets here.'

FIFTH SUNDAY OF EASTER

Equal Opportunities

Acts 11:1-18

Equal opportunities
is politically correct;
a must in every business plan
a buzzword at every union meeting
essential to education and employment policy –
a laudable attempt to iron out the playing field.

It is also a myth, a threat, a misguided, misleading delusion.

Isn't it?

We are not equal:
nor indifferent to our own interest. Neither, then,
can our opportunities be equal.

For every orphan rescued by the international charity
and trained in medicine or law
there will be a hundred thousand more
whose dreams die with them in the camp.

I cannot go to Oxbridge;
not because I come from a state school/ethnic minority/poor home
but because I don't have the confidence to cope with the tutorial system
and won't get straight A's.

She cannot join the Fire Service
not because she is female
but because she is too feeble to lift an unconscious body
and has no head for heights.

He cannot buy this property
not because he is black

but because the chain broke down and, under our crazy system,
someone else got there first.

I am not equal to you in brains or beauty
in wealth or wisdom
in religion or race
in strengths or weaknesses, opportunities, threats
or in any other sort of analysis.

We are equal only before God.

Before one another, we jockey for position,
defend our corner, claim our rights,
give in to feelings of superiority – or inferiority:
react to differences by flight or fight.

So it is that, lacking love, we have recourse to law:
the Equal Opportunities Commission
the Sex Discrimination Act
the Commission for Racial Equality
the Disability Act:
all there to prevent us from giving in to our baser instincts
to tell us to treat Jew and Gentile, slave and free, male and female alike;
all there to make us love one another as Jesus loved us
or at least, Act like we did.

But let's not deceive ourselves: there are no short cuts
to building heaven on earth.
Remember, Jesus said,
'The poor you will always have with you . . .'
He knew human nature too well to believe
that the law could do anything other than bring us to him,
crying out in frustration,
crying out in despair,
crying out for new birth,
crying out for the Spirit of love;
and it seems he did not much care
that this world is unequal, unfair.

Perhaps we have to discover in each generation
that where love is lacking
law may be needed
but it serves only to show us again
our lack of love.

Wouldn't it be great if we had more acts of God
and fewer Acts of Parliament?
Love dispensed instead of laws,
people responding from the heart
instead of under duress?

But already it has begun,
the love of God poured out at Pentecost
not just upon his chosen Jewish nation
but broadcast to every tribe and tongue;
and Peter sees, and understands
that *there* is an equal opportunity for all,
salvation being free, and freely offered
equally,
without prejudice
without qualification
except a man be thirsty for it.

Let no one ever say our God is exclusive!

And one day, we will know the liberation
of true equality
when I am not threatened by your opportunity
and you are not weakened by my success;

for the love of God is the matrix
on which the new heaven and the new earth are designed
and the stuff from which they are built;
and the sea of uncertainty,
the sea of insecurity and fear,
the waves of violence and self-interest
that swell and break the surface under threat –
all will be gone and,

in the presence of God,
we will know ourselves
equally valued,
equally, perfectly loved,
equally special;

finally
naturally
supernaturally
we will love one another as Jesus loves us
and find ourselves
equally satisfied.

SIXTH SUNDAY OF EASTER

Down by the Riverside

Acts 16:9-15; Revelation 21:10, 22–22:5; John 5:1-9

Why do I dream of a house
with a stream at the bottom of the garden?
Why, when we moved office,
did my boss insist on a fountain by the door?
Why can we sit on a beach
and stare for hours at the sea?

Why did Lydia and the other ladies
choose a river for their place of prayer?
Why did the suffering
wait expectantly by a pool?
Why is there
a major water feature in the new Jerusalem?

Earth, air, fire – and water;
this, truly, is back to basics:
the elemental nature of God
speaking to what is deepest in man.

Water, speaking of boundaries,
defendable frontier
safe haven
moated existence.

But boundaries are there to be crossed.
Once the Euphrates marked the end of the known world;
Alexander's armies stopped short for fear of falling off the edge
until their leader crossed, showing the way to push back the boundaries,
expand the empire eastward.
Once the Dardanelles marked the end of the Christian world;

Paul and his companions stopped short in Troas, wondering
until their Lord gave the vision, showing the way to push back the
boundaries,
expand the Kingdom westward.

Yes, boundaries are sometimes there to be crossed;
which side of the water am I?
The familiar, homeward side
or the unknown territory, over among the lost?
Can my Lord trust me with his dreams,
trust me to catch the next tide?

Water, speaking too of washing,
ceremonial
stain removal,
fresh start.

But washing is merely the outward sign.
Pilate tried by washing his hands to escape the guilt of a death;
Lady Macbeth tried it too, and realised it couldn't be done.
Of all who have tried to wash their hands of responsibility
none has emerged clean;
but if the ladies of Philippi chose to meet by the river
in order to wash and pray, in the Jewish way, as best they knew,
at least they were in the best place to learn of the water of life
and a baptism which would last for ever.

When the outward sign
is more than an outward show
performed through fear, superstition or pride –
when the outward sign
is the sacrament of a contrite heart,
God is down by the riverside.

Water, speaking too of change –
current affairs
go with the flow
never step in the same river twice.

I need to know that all can be made new.
Every wave has a life of its own, building, balancing, breaking,
leaving its own unique signature on the beach;
perhaps this next one will bring me a fish, or a friend
or sweep me away from the plodding path I was taking;
and if the suffering agreed to wait by a pool, the best they knew,
in order to catch that wave which somehow gave them a fresh start,
at least they were in the best place, a place of acknowledged need
to meet the Son of God who came to impart life to the full.

The sound of water is never the same: improvisation
of a master musician. I cannot tear myself away,
I must know what is coming next –
the movement convinces me something is moving in my life
or may yet move. As long as the water flows, re-creation
is possible, all things are possible:

surely I can lay down my burden, refuse to study war,
mend a few bridges, pan for gold?

Here, down by the riverside
I long for my life to flow like the stream,
overflow like the fountain,
swell like the sea;
never to run dry
never to seize up
never to ebb away from me.

Here, down by the riverside
I long for my life to break out from its boundaries,
wash its slate,
change from the inside out;
never to be constrained, except by you,
never to let the dust settle, except on sin forgiven,
never to rest content, except with your likeness.

But only there, up by your heavenly riverside
there, where the angels light
on the bright river,
river of life, sprung from the very throne of God,
will these things come to be.

ASCENSION

Right-hand Man

Daniel 7:9-14; Psalm 47; Ephesians 1:15-23

Once, beyond time,
there was an old, old king,
old as the universe itself at least, because he made it; maybe older,
who knows what happens beyond time?
The king sat in his splendid throne room, called heaven,
resting his feet lightly on his footstool, called earth
which was a bit groaning and rickety:
one of these days he'd get a new one
or, being ecologically minded,
recycle what could be saved from the old one.

Meanwhile in the school playground
two small boys, me and my friend, argue the toss:
'I'm bigger than you, I can beat you up!'
'But my dad's better than yours, he's got a new 4 x 4.'
'Well, we've got a – a – private plane and a pet panda and broadband!'
'We own a whole Disneyworld!'
'Well, we own the whole world, so there!'
'We own the stars and the moon and the whole universe!'
And on, and on, upping the ante until the bell rings
and we come down to earth with a bump.

The old king clears his throat
'Excuse me,' he says politely,
'don't I come into this somewhere?'
But the boys hear only the sound of their own voices
rehearsing tomorrow's round.
And the old king weeps a torrent of tears
as he sends for his Son, signing him up
as his secret – and not so secret – agent on earth,
seeking whatever can be saved
by signing his own death warrant.

Meanwhile the two small boys, me and my friend
argue on in the playground.

'You know, we don't really own the world,' I say. 'God does.'

'I don't think there *is* a God,' says my friend,
'because look, if there *was* an old man with a long white beard
sitting up there on a cloud,
well, he'd fall through, see?
Bound to – clouds are only lots of drops of water,
my dad told me.
So, I don't think there *is* a God!'

'Old man?' I say
'Long white beard?' I say.
'Sitting on a cloud?' I say.
'You must be daft! Bonkers! Loony-balloony!'
And I fall about laughing.

'What's so funny?' says my friend. 'I thought you believed in God!'

'Oh, I do,' I say. 'But not a cartoon God – the *real* one.'

'Oh yeah?' says my friend. 'So, what did *he* do?'

'He made the world,' I say. 'He's great!'

'Oh yeah?' says my friend. 'That was some time ago; and then?'

'He divided the Red Sea to save his people,' I say. 'He's great!'

'Oh yeah,' says my friend. 'That was some time ago; and then?'

'He sent his son Jesus to save the world,' I say. 'He worked miracles, healed people – he's great!'

'Oh yeah?' says my friend. 'That was some time ago; and then?'

'Jesus died,' I say, 'but God raised him from the dead – he's great!'

'Oh yeah?' says my friend. 'That was some time ago, too – and *now*?'
He leans forward and grabs my sweatshirt.
'And *now*?' he says, 'What's he doing *now*, then?'

The old king clears his throat.
'Excuse me,' he says politely,
'I think I may be able to help you there.'
The boys spin round, but see only the school caretaker
sweeping up dirt and leaves.
'Jesus was once a small boy too,' the caretaker says,
'the only boy who could truly boast about owning the world
probably never did! But God raised him up from the dead
to do just that – to take his divine power
and rule, over all that there is: for God said,

"I need my son at my side
and the earth needs a new king;
I need to set before them a saviour
that all the world can sing;
I need a right-hand man
and the church needs a head;
I need a just and merciful judge
for the living and the dead.

"So come! come up higher, Jesus,
sit down at my right hand;
come where the universe can see
that you, a man they can understand
(not some vague deity or force),
you I've made Lord of all creation.
Commander-in-chief of heaven's troops,
ruler of every tribe and nation."'

'What's Jesus doing now?'
The caretaker scratched his ear.
'I reckon he's busy enough;
after all, he not only owns the world
but the stars and the moon and the whole universe!

He said that when he was lifted up,
he would draw everyone to himself:
so that's what he's doing,
praying for them to come and be saved,
sending his Holy Spirit to challenge and cheer.
Kings and dictators, princes and presidents,
earthly and spiritual powers, they'll all come:
willing or not (and he prays they may be willing),
every knee will bow, every tongue confess
that indeed he *is* great: the greatest!

'And he cares and prays for you too,
you and your friend.' He looked at his watch.
'Away with the pair of you now!
He may have a world to rule
but I have a school to take care of!'

High above, larks are singing
in exultation;
the old king, and his son, and his caretaking spirit
smile at the two boys
and the song of re-creation.

SEVENTH SUNDAY OF EASTER

Chain Reaction

Acts 16:16-34

It all began with the slave girl
chained not only to her owner
but to that spirit,
spirit of Apollo
python spirit
demon spirit
whispering the future to the fearful,
infiltrating, insinuating,
taking control,
making as well as telling fortunes
to line her master's pocket . . .

Poor girl, locked into a life of abuse
of body, mind and spirit:
or is she?
With God, every prediction can be shattered,
every chain broken:
nothing inevitable except his dying, and undying love.

Then the next link in the chain,
her owner – chained himself
to the demon greed
breeding anger
breeding violence
breeding lies;
seizing hold of the innocent,
abusing, falsely accusing,
inciting hatred,
inviting prejudice
all to mask his love of Mammon.

Rich man, but locked in a vice,
heart and conscience clamped:
or is he?
God has paid the price of our self-interest,
broken every chain:
each of us can be stamped with the seal of his ownership –
if such is our will.

And then, a tangle of links:
the crowd, chained as always
to feelings, swayed
by unlaid ghosts,
chat show hosts,
potential votes;
protesting their rights:
Hey! Join the fray!
Finding a voice,
finding a moment of meaning
to punctuate their monotone life's sentence.

Fickle crowd! Locked into the to and fro
of maverick emotion:
or are they?
With God, every deceitful heart can be stilled,
every chain broken;
he can be the measure of their mind and the anchor of their soul.

And now, the magistrates,
the Roman praetors, chained
to their office,
judging not without fear or favour
judging rather from fear of reprisals
judging to favour political masters,
ignoring the need for evidence.
Beat'em now, ask'em later!
Out of sight,
out of mind:
law and order at any price . . .

Rough justice! Locked into the system
of might is right:
or are they?
With God, all pursuit of power can be checked,
every chain broken;
only those who bow the knee to Christ will be allowed to rule.

And so to another tangle, this time
of prisoners, chained
by their feet, their clay feet
because of wickedness,
weakness
ignorance
reaping just or unjust rewards,
deserving or undeserving,
ganged up
banged up
bound by the strong Roman arm of the law.

Captives! Locked not only in cells
but into wrongdoing:
or are they?
With God, every failure can be forgiven,
every chain broken;
we fell foul of the law but he was sentenced;
the door to heaven is open.

And so to the final link,
the jailer, chained
by the chance of being an underling:
not worth the risk
jobsworth
much as my life is worth
got to keep the bosses happy
locks, stocks
key carrying
card carrying
don't blame him, he's only doing his job.

Little man! Locked in by the everyday pressures
of keeping a wife and kids;
or is he?
With God, all vulnerability can be reassured,
every chain broken:
he has promised to keep us safe, and keeps his word.

Links in a chain, a chain of events:
but what will it take to trigger the chain reaction?

First, take a man of God
filled with the Spirit of God
filled with the fire of God:
then, send him into the situation,
light the blue touch paper, and blow your mind

for demons are recognised
and exorcised; all hell is let loose as injustice has her way
for a day; men who are bleeding and sore
and should surely be broken, shout for joy and pray and sing
and the earth quakes and breaks iron
but prisoners refuse to escape, the jailer's persuaded to stay his sword,
stay to hear the way of salvation
the way to enjoy a freedom that flies in the face
of abuse
and greed
and self-interest,
injustice and weakness and vulnerability –

and every chain is broken
as every man, woman and child
is invited to be washed clean,
to come, and sit and eat,
to be filled with joy
and to walk free.

PENTECOST

Strong Language

Genesis 11:1-9; Acts 2:1-21

I used to be vaguely amused
by all those minority groups who fought to preserve
their ancient language
but I'm beginning to wonder
whether, in fact, God may be on the side of the Gaelic speakers,
the Cornish, the Irish and even
Plaid Cymru with their pots of green paint to airbrush the English;

it was he, after all, who came up with the notion,
that original ingenious, non-violent solution,
to check our overweening ambition,
understanding that greater communication
meant greater cooperation,
for good or ill:
too much for men to handle
without trespassing
on the property of God.

Shared words
shared knowledge
giving us ideas above our station,
belief in our own, boundless powers of creation,
raising us in our own estimation
to think that, having described a thing
we have mastered it;
having constructed it in words
sooner or later,
we will construct it in reality:
alchemy *will* one day turn base metal to gold.
Knowledge, once tasted, cannot be contained,
neither controlled.

Eden is ended,
nothing is now beyond our reach;
nothing is sacred.

Such pride, though, has no place in heaven,
shading, as it does
an angel of light into the Prince of Darkness;
not only did God pitch Lucifer out,
he also, for good measure,
tossed a spanner into the building works
of the tower which tempted,
attempted
the throne of God:
a spanner called confusion,
babble, Babel, Babylon,
gate of a pretender's heaven.

Creating man with so much potential
certainly gave the Almighty grief
and the need, on occasion,
to use strong language;
'Out! Out of Eden, and shut the gate behind you!'
'Let it rain, let it flood the earth and drown your wickedness!'
'Away with you, to the ends of the earth,
and reinvent the wheel in your own words!'
Exile, death, division –
better than godless living.

And it has taken many travellers,
linguists, philologists, interpreters,
translators, indexers and scribes,
not to mention empire builders
many, many years
to link the minds which words
more than worlds,
divide . . .

. . . to such a point that now I fear
for all us English speakers, now we have
not just the legacy of empire

but pride of place on the computer screen,
a voice across the world –
what might we plan? How conspire? To what aspire?
Can we be trusted?
Or will we wake up one morning
to find ourselves victims of some divine virus,
our wires crossed
our codes scrambled
our neighbours talking double Dutch
(all right, you might think it has happened already
to look at the average help screen
or business plan),
but seriously,
would God do it again?

Yes, he wants his people to be one
but his ways are not our ways.
Understanding came
not from years spent in a language lab,
dictionary in one hand, grammar in the other
but, when he willed it,
when we were ready,
in a flash of flame
by a breath of wind
on wings of prayer:
communication
with all the scattered sons of Shem, Ham and Japheth
in an instant;
not by might, nor by power
but by my Spirit, and for my purpose,
says the Lord

who plans to unite all things
only
in Christ.

So watch your language, child,
make sure your tongue doesn't trip you,
or your words run away with you,

your rhetoric with your reason,
your pride with your passion;
for only words inspired by the Spirit of God
build us together as children of God,
through grace, not works,
in case we should boast and God be forced to prove, again,
that pride comes before destruction,
and we approach the Most High
only through the towering mercy
of Christ.

Watch your language, child
and do not try to reach heaven from earth,
to rival God or pull him down –
no need! For Babel is reversed at Pentecost:
God has come down to earth from heaven,
speaking to each
in the strong universal language of love:
'Come to me! Be one with me!'

So may your words be
yes! and
Amen! and
Jesus Christ is Lord!

Ordinary Time

TRINITY SUNDAY

So, Who Wants To Know?

Psalm 8

What is man, that you are mindful of him,
the son of man, that you care for him?

So, who wants to know?

Tell the biologist
I'm *homo sapiens*, an erect biped
with a highly developed brain (what, all of us?)
powers of articulate speech,
abstract reasoning and imagination (what, all of us?)

Tell the chemist
I'm mostly water (what, no alcohol?)
fat – enough for seven bars of soap
sugar – to sweeten seven teas
lime – enough to coat a chicken coop
sulphur to rid a single dog of fleas;
a few other additives,
not much in the way of preservatives, hopefully no E numbers.

Tell the astronomer
I'm a speck of dust on a medium-sized planet
orbiting an undistinguished star,
one in a million or so.

Tell the doctor
I'm a fertilised egg stroke embryo stroke viable foetus
and I object to being aborted stroke terminated stroke killed;
I feel I am neither too young nor too old nor too ill
to place myself unreservedly
at the mercy of your new-found, controversial skill.

Tell the evolutionist
there are dozens of missing links in his chain
and whilst I may share quite a bit of my DNA
with the chimpanzee, I feel essentially, distinctly, *me.*

And tell my wife
that I'm the one who's going down the pub
to watch the big match
again.
I'll be back at ten
and I do love her really.

What is man?
Surely the very fact that I ask the question
points to the answer . . . I am different,
different enough to be aware of the difference,
different enough to compare myself with the bear
or the chair or the pear, which simply accept their place
in the grand scheme of things
(or the grand randomness of things, if you go with the big bang);
different enough to *want* to ask what
and who
and why?

And I ask not
as a biologist, chemist or astronomer; not
as a doctor or husband, even;
this is not some technical, academic question
about classification, statistics or even role
but a cry from the heart
about meaning, and purpose and soul (if there is such a thing).

I am the business tycoon with four yachts
and as many broken marriages;
I am the fisherman whose boat and baby were lost in the flood;
I am the bored and pointless bureaucrat;
I am the child soldier forced at gunpoint to taste blood.

I am all of these, and none; I am all – and nothing; I am legion,
I am dust.

In all this teeming world
outside and inside my mind
is there one whose voice will slice through the cacophony
and tell me, unequivocally,
what is mankind
and who am I?

There is One
who is also three
who said to himself, 'Let us make man in our image'.

I am *made,* then, not man-made, self-made,
and certainly no accident
but made by God
who saw everything he had created, and rated it
ten out of ten.

I am made
in the image of God the Father,
made in the image of the Father, to raise up children for him;
made in the image of the Creator, to create, thinking his thoughts
  after him and crafting them into being;
made in the image of the Sovereign Lord,
  to rule with authority and grace the animate and inanimate
  kingdoms in his name.

I am made
in the image of God the Son,
made in the image of the Son, to be first and foremost a child of God
born into his family not by my parents' choice, but by my decision;
all my life a child of my Father, secure in his love and provision
but sharing too the call of his first-born Son, to be
that suffering servant.

I am made
in the image of God the Holy Spirit,
made in the image of the Spirit, offering me the wisdom of God,
inspiring me to stand by his side, see what he's doing, allow his love
to work through me, feel his joy in the sheer amazingness of it all,

share his delight in man. What?
His delight in *me*? Surely not.

What is God, that he is mindful of me,
the Son of God, that he cares for me?

I alone am the one
called by my Lord to share his heart, to cry his tears,
to speak with his tongue, bless with his hands,
in the power of his Spirit to beat my spears
into garden forks, my bombs into airlifts of aid,
my poisoned darts of gossip into lines of love –
called, yes, to be one day crowned with glory and honour;

but I am also the one
who until that day is a battlefield
where the Father, the Son and the Holy Spirit within me fight
to the death with the man who would live for the moment
against the day,
planting for pleasure,
ruthlessly reaping the world's riches,
storing up status symbols till they shut out the light.

What a mass of contradictions is this poor man!
At the flick of a switch
I sound the heights or the depths
but, against all expectation, beyond all reason,
because you have said it, this
I hold on to,
this:

that you *are* mindful of me, you *do* care for me, and more:
I am precious in your sight
and honoured
and you love me.

PROPER 4

World's End

1 Kings 18:22-23, 41-43; Psalm 96:1-9; Luke 7:1-10

My reverend grandfather
would say, waving his pipe expansively,
that his parish reached to the World's End:
he had in mind
the pub in Chelsea,
but it was a good line.

Perhaps the ends of the earth
do not have such a daunting ring
in these days of cut-price flights,
gap years, compulsive globe-trotting:
The Hitchhiker's Guide to the Galaxy
says it all,

  though for the most part
  we still prefer our hotels to be finished,
  our treks to be guided, our luggage carried,
  our time under canvas with no mod cons
  to be limited, the menu to be varied
  and in English –

but *then* – when there was no such thing
as short-term mission;
when you set sail for the world's end
with a one-way ticket; when health
and wealth, family and friends
were laid on the line –

what was it, then, that so captivated
the hearts and minds of so many men,
the Hudson Taylors, C. T. Studds,
the Cambridge Seven, and sent them

to the furthest, most alien parts
of the known world?

What was it, then, that so fascinated
the young John Coleridge Patteson
that he left our tiny country village
for an early grave in the South Pacific?
Why would he not be a poet,
like his uncle?

Today, we get on a plane
and expect to arrive tomorrow
on the other side of the world,
suitably wined and dined in transit:
the only inconvenience
a touch of jet lag.

Then, to get on a ship
heralded weeks and months
of uncertain health, weather and food;
little communication, even less assurance
of safe landing, or of the mood
of the natives.

What was it, then, that gave them
such faraway dreams, such a deaf ear
to the cries of creature comforts
and quiet lives? What strange gravity
drew their will, wrote their life sentence,
fulfilled their fears – and hopes?

David and Solomon glimpsed it:
that Israel's God – did it seem like arrogance? –
was no mere locality manager:
rather, a multi-national power
making a take-over bid for the hearts
of the whole world,

    and the whole world
    would surely come – did it seem like arrogance? –

knocking at their door, knocking
at the temple door, to find out more
of the God whose outstretched arm
circled the earth,

spun the planets,
the God whose hand
crafted whatever his mind's eye
could conjure; the God whose name
alone should light, and delight
heaven and earth;

the God whose heart
blazed with a love that overflowed
the boundaries of Israel, finally
pouring itself into the human form
of his Son, greater than any temple,
imploring 'Ask . . . seek . . . knock . . .'

And so the rumour of deity spread
and through the ages they came:
the Sassenachs, the outsiders
the Queen of Sheba, the proselytes,
the faithful centurion, seeking out
God and his Son.

But whereas to the outsiders
Jesus said 'Come!'
to the disciples he then said 'Go!
Go to the world's end, where there are still
unreached lands; go to the world's end
while there is still time.'

Why, then? Why does the name,
and the hand and the outstretched arm
and the heart of God fail
to galvanise my hands, and feet,
my heart and will as it did
those missionary saints?

Why, when the world has shrunk
to what might seem a rather more
manageable size, has our vision,
our nerve, our imagination
also shrunk to be such a tentative,
brittle thing?

The solidity of our structures belies
the fragility of our faith;
we neither foresee the faithless
flocking to join us, coming to knock on our door,
nor dare to hear the whispered

'*Go* . . . and join them, knock on their door.

'*Listen* . . . until you hear the cry
of their heart, untouched
by the idle words of their gods;
look . . . until you discern the space
between human searching
and God's finding

'and dare to claim that ground:
till every foreigner knows
that I am no foreign God, but their own
soul's home; and you will know
there are no foreigners: all are one in Christ!

Glory be to the Father, and to the Son,
and to the Holy Spirit: as it was in the beginning,
is now, and ever shall be: world without end. Amen!'

PROPER 5

You Can't Argue with That

1 Kings 17:17-24; Galatians 1:11-24; Luke 7:11-17

Of course, anyone can *say*
that they have the ear of God,
that they know the mind of God,
that they speak with the voice of God –
but how do we know?

There are so many voices,
so many so-called gods
and no-gods; anything from avocados
to Zen can be seen as the answer:
so how do we know?

The widow of Zarephath
already had her jar of meal
and her jug of oil supernaturally filled:
but who, really, was this guy Elijah
if her son could be killed?

Where was God in all of that? Suddenly, there –
when Elijah took him upstairs and prayed
and the boy sat up and drew breath,
then she knew him to be a true man of God:
only God can bring life from death.

You can't argue with that.

And that other widow, from Nain:
who knows if she'd even heard of Jesus
or what God meant to her?
All she saw was a bier and a bleak horizon
through a blur of tears;

no one to care for her now,
now that her son was dead:
where was God in all of that? Suddenly, there –
in the one who touched his coffin, and said 'Get up!'
Only God can bring life from death.

You can't argue with that.

And only God can bring spiritual life
from spiritual death:

you can't argue with that, either.

Oh, but we do –
we do when it comes to Paul, don't we?
Jesus, yes! we say, great;
but Paul? No thanks!
Jesus teaches in words of one syllable;
Paul uses words like 'justification'.
Jesus is nice and straightforward;
Paul just complicates everything.
Jesus speaks across the ages;
Paul is caught in his own culture.
Jesus valued women;
Paul is a male chauvinist pig.

We'll just stick to the Gospels, and
thank heaven all those letters
weren't written to *us:*
just who did Paul think he was, anyway?

Well, he thought he was an Apostle
and if he was
then all those letters *were,* in a way, written to us
who claim to follow the Apostles' teaching.

Saul of Tarsus,
dead keen on the letter of the law,
dead against Christians,

dead set on destroying them;
despite his sincerity
dead wrong.

Where was God in all of that? Suddenly, there –
there in a blinding flash on a desert road
lighting the truth that religion had obscured,
igniting that spark of new life:
only God can bring spiritual life from spiritual death.

You can't argue with that.

Even Saul, master of logic, rhetoric
and theological debate
was not inclined to argue with that; instead
he goes away for three whole years
to clear his conscience,
revise his opinions,
listen to his new-found Lord,
listen to those three years of incredible wisdom
shared with the twelve, and now with him;
listen to the law distilled, and fulfilled
in the one whose followers he killed;
listen to his own great commission
to go into all the world and preach the gospel.

And with what dynamic life he returned!
With what tireless energy he travelled,
with what patient faith he faced persecution,
with what passion did he defend the one true gospel:
the gospel not gleaned from others,
no second-hand sermons
but revealed by the living Lord Jesus himself to Paul,
last but not least of the great Apostles.

Or so he says.

Of course, anyone can *say*
that they have the ear of God,

that they know the mind of God,
that they speak with the voice of God –
but how do we *know*?

How do we know
that Paul received his commission
to work and witness, speak
and write
from the risen Lord himself?
That we must come to all of Scripture
not in fight or flight, but
in submission?

Finally, it is faith:
but faith based on evidence
of life from death;
physical life restored
foreshadows the regeneration
of spiritual life, the transformation
of Saul and the other Apostles,
the transformation of millions since,
the beginnings of transformation
even in me
as I hear, and receive the gospel of Christ
according to Paul.

Only God can bring life from death.

I can't argue with that.

PROPER 6

Big Sinner, Little Sinner

2 Samuel 11:26–12:10, 13-15; Psalm 32; Galatians 2:15-21; Luke 7:36–8:3

LS Excuse me, I think I may have come to the wrong place!

BS Really?

LS I'm not sure I really belong among such – distinguished company.

BS Come, come: I'm sure you underestimate yourself!

LS No, no, I assure you: compared with your *major* contributions
of adultery, deceit, murder, prostitution,
anything I could offer is a mere peccadillo,
a trifle, an error of judgement, a momentary lapse:
hardly a sin demanding absolution.

BS You are too modest a fellow.

LS No, no: I am confessing that not only have I murdered no one,
but I hate no one; sure, there are a few folk I'd rather not meet,
rather not cross the street for, that's only natural – but hate?
No, no.

BS And adultery . . . ?

LS Never! Don't even think about it.

BS Really? Deceit? The heart is deceitful above all things.

LS You should know . . .

BS I do know. I'm under no illusions
about the gap, the great gap
between what I am and what I ought to be;

my sins, as God would have it, are splashed across the tabloids
for all to see and point the finger: and believe themselves
secure in the delusion of their greater rectitude.

LS I trust you don't include me in your speculation!
I am not, I think, deluded, in my estimation.

BS How, then, do you estimate?

LS Well, I was baptised soon after I was born,
and have been pretty faithful ever since;
apart from a brief flirtation with Buddhism,
I've never strayed from the fold.
I don't smoke, or swear, or 'drink and drive'
or search the internet for porn
or covet my kid brother's gold card.
I hurt no one, I try to lend a helping hand –
in short, a law-abiding citizen,
leading a good Christian life.

BS And how, I wonder, does God estimate?

LS Eh?

BS Law-abiding, yes, that's what they all say,
all the great faiths: lose yourself, respect nature,
pray daily, give to the poor, honour the dead:
do this, don't do that – try hard, and maybe the gods, if they exist,
will smile on you.

LS Jesus too. Jesus didn't come to abolish the law . . .

BS . . . but to fulfil it! Don't you see,
he came to do what *only* he could do – fulfil it!
God is looking for men after his own heart:
not men who read the rulebook
like a schoolboy reads his homework diary,
but men whose hearts are overflowing with the love of God,
whose lives leave the rulebook standing,
lives like a fiery sun burning up a picture of the sun,

like being served a ten-course banquet
rather than being handed a recipe.

LS Bit extravagant . . .

BS Extravagant, yes, that's it!
Love God with all my heart, soul, mind and strength
and the law will look after itself.
Labouring to keep God's law, without God's life and love
is fruitless, faithless – and, in the end, fatal.

LS Oh, come on! That's going too far;
you just want a licence for – licence.

BS No, no! I am gutted by my failures, my betrayals;
and yet, because of them, I have tasted
the wonder of my Father's forgiveness,
kindling again that fire of love in my heart,
love for him which knows no calculation,
throws caution to the winds in one great,
all-embracing celebration!
Little Sinner,
you say you do not hate – but tell me,
do you love? How much
or how little?
To lead a good, Christian life,
is this not to be known for our extravagant love,
poured out like perfume on precious feet,
for our profligate spending of time and talents
to bring God glory?
Is this not to be known for our ready forgiveness,
for counting one another better than ourselves,
for unbounded confidence and undying trust
in the grace and mercy of God?

LS All this sounds like rather an extreme sport;
my religion is perhaps rather more – English;
more of an agreement between gentlemen.
Play by the rules, and your fingers won't get burned.

BS I fear that God is more than a gentleman
and we are less.

LS Speak for yourself!

BS I do. I know I have not earned heaven,
do not deserve my destiny as a child of God;
my most worthy works are marred by mixed motives
and intimations of pride. 'By the works of the law
can no man living be justified . . .'
Why else should Christ die?

LS It comes to us all.

BS Indeed. And after that, judgement. Lord, have mercy on us,
for we have all sinned and fallen short of your glory!

LS Though some of us are only little sinners . . .

BS My friend, still you underestimate yourself:
there are no degrees of sin,
only of understanding of sin.

PROPER 7

Pigs Might Fly

Luke 8:26-39

You know the most bizarre thing
about this whole, bizarre story?
That while the madman raged naked round the tombs
and, breaking his chains, went rampaging, screaming,
terrorising the neighbourhood –
they were not, it seems,
terrorised;
only
when he was cured.

I am glad, Luke, that you're such a reliable type
with your doctor's powers of observation,
    probing beneath the surface of things,
    noting the detail, the aberration, what signifies;
with your historian's meticulous mind
    researching, tracking down witnesses,
    checking your sources, ordering, making sense . . .
Coming from anyone else,
it might be all too easy to dismiss
this whole episode as melodramatic
flight of fancy, or at best
exaggeration –

but no.
It is all part of your chapter of thorough examination
of the claim of the Saviour of the world
to deliver us from evil,
from all evil:
from the evil of the storm on the lake –
    circumstances which buffet and bruise and break,
    circumstances over which we have no control;

from the evil of weakness and ill health
    like the woman bleeding for twelve years,
    like all of us who are but dust;
from the evil, the final evil of death
    the last enemy, who claimed Jairus' daughter,
    the last enemy, with his so-called winning card;
and here, from the evil that attacks our very minds,
    legion our disorders, fears and phobias,
    legion the demonic influences, still.

Yes, deliver us from evil,
from all these evils:
not that we will no longer face them –
you write precisely to show us that we will –
but they will not overcome us.

True, our victory may be a long time coming,
our arms pulled almost from their sockets with hanging on.
Not every storm is stilled – yet:
    not every flood or earthquake caused by ignorance or greed,
    and Paul was storm-tossed, shipwrecked more than once.
Not everyone is healed – yet:
    suffering does not always lead to saintliness
    and Timothy and Paul lived with their 'thorns'.
Not everyone is raised from death – yet:
    most Christians die, never again to walk here
    and resurrection is a matter of faith.

It seems, though, that wherever,
whenever the demonic made itself known
Jesus responded in no uncertain terms
to a challenge thrown down which he could not refuse:
evil revealed
without ambiguity or disguise
must be shown who's master;
Satan must not be allowed to steal
our free will to choose,
be it for good or ill.

So what of this drama, Luke,
this well-researched melodrama?
Demons? Surely not, in this day and age.
Well, I don't know what the day or the age have to do with it;
it was either true then, *and* now
or never –
though Satan would be more than pleased
to see us fall into either of those equal and opposite errors:
to believe he is responsible for everything
or nothing; more than pleased
to see us duped by every docu-soap on exorcism
or, in our eyes, allow them to discredit the whole thing.
And we are pleased to oblige,
just like those Galileans in the madman's town
dismissing the claims,
dismissing the evidence,
throwing the newly delivered baby out with the bathwater.

What were they afraid of?
What are we afraid of?

We are accustomed to a certain evil,
we can accommodate it, more or less:
a domestic evil, a common selfishness, or pride,
even betrayal – this is 'part of life's rich tapestry'
and when it comes to crime against society,
why, we have the law to shield us from the fall-out,
tidy the streets, close the door.

But suddenly,
the children fighting with wooden swords hear
the crying of the man down the road whose son was killed in Iraq;

just as the citizens of Galilee see, for a moment,
the curtain twitched aside to show
the greater evil behind the less.

Evil behind evils
the shadow of our mundane struggles thrown,

grotesque, onto the screen of that cosmic struggle
of which they *do* form part – principalities and powers,
Michael and all his angels against the powers of darkness,
and this is not the stuff of fantasy or war-game;
this is more real than anything:

something
got into those pigs and sent them flying to destruction.

No wonder the people were afraid . . .

And sometimes it makes me wonder if it could be
the same something that 'got into' my friend's husband
when he suddenly upped and left her, with harsh, strange words;
the same something that made the young man 'beside himself'
with an uncontrollable desire to draw blood;
the same something that made the doctor say, 'She "wasn't herself",
hadn't been for several months before her suicide.'

And I could be afraid . . .

But don't let us forget, Luke,
that you wrote precisely to show us, that
although we will face evils
and maybe Evil,
it will not overcome us; yes,
Satan is the Prince of this world – who fights tooth and nail
but with the desperation of one who knows that his number is up;
and it is *Jesus* to whom all authority in heaven
and on earth is finally given,
Jesus who lives in us:

and he who is in us
is greater than he who is in the world

and he said 'Don't be afraid . . .'

PROPER 8

Just a Minute . . .

1 Kings 19:15, 16, 19-21; Psalm 16; Luke 9:51-62

Just a minute, Lord:
I will follow you, sure I will,
but just let me see the summer out with my girlfriend,
check out the Buddhist retreat, just to make sure
it doesn't suit me better,
wait till my mate moves to France, he thinks
Christians are creeps –
then I will follow you, sure I will!

But Jesus turned and looked at me over his shoulder
'You,' he said, 'follow me
without hesitation, deviation, or repetition
of any of those lame excuses!'

Just a minute, Lord:
I will follow you, sure I will
but just let me wait till my dad is on the mend,
the Sunday league is over
and the local church gets a new vicar
because the present one
is *female*, and looks like the back of a bus –
then I will follow you, sure I will!

But Jesus turned and looked at me again, a little sad:
'You know the rules,' he said,
'and you lose three points: for hesitation,
deviation and repetition of lame excuses!'

Just a minute, though, Lord:
when Elijah called Elisha to follow,
throwing his cloak around him

Elisha was allowed to go back, first to kiss
his father and mother goodbye;
why, he could even have absconded
with the prophet's cloak! But Elijah
trusted him . . . So why should I miss out?

But Jesus said 'I know, remember, what is in men's hearts;
Elisha's going back was only to kill his oxen,
break his plough, burn his boats: all to ensure
there was *no* going back. And you?'

Just a minute, Lord:
Are you saying that once I decide
to follow you, there's no way
I can change my mind?
But it's hard to be sure until you've tried.
What if I find I'm wrong? I'd rather pay
an annual subscription than apply
for life membership.

But Jesus shook his head and said 'I'm afraid it's life
we're talking about here: take it or leave it.
By all means count the cost: the ticket's free,
but the run could be quite – demanding.'

Just a minute, Lord:
demanding? That reminds me of the night-time
training when we were told to follow
the rope laid across country, straight through
bogs and brambles, rivers and rocks
and we sank in mud and froze in the ice-cold water
and bled from a thousand thorns
and all in the pitch dark.

But Jesus smiled and said 'Exactly: but the rope held
and as long as you held the rope
you were safe; you finished your course
and survived to tell the tale.'

Just a minute, Lord:
are you telling me life with you is like that?
An obstacle course with no concessions
for good behaviour, take what comes,
just hold the rope, hold on to the rope
and keep going, keep going, don't look back
don't give in to your fears and whatever you do:
don't let go!

And Jesus smiled again and said 'That's a pretty good summary
at least of the night times; think, though
that as long as you hold on to me, there's nothing that
can stop you: nothing you cannot come through.'

Just a minute, Lord:
I remember another time,
a high mountain ridge, with a drop
of a thousand feet to left and right
and a track a few inches wide
and I thought 'Never in a million years . . .' and froze inside.
But I fixed my gaze on the man in front
and did what I couldn't do.

And Jesus, son of David, repeated David's words
'I have set the Lord before me;
because he is at my right hand,
I shall not be shaken.'

Just a minute, Lord:
are you saying it's more important
to have a guide than to have a map?
That it doesn't matter what you go through
or how long it takes, or what state you arrive in
provided you've hung on in there
and we end up still together –
goodness, that sounds a bit like marriage!

And Jesus said, 'Hmm, not a bad analogy; after all,
when you've found the right person, you don't hesitate,

deviate into red-light districts or repeatedly
prevaricate – you normally can't wait!'

Just a minute, Lord:
I know that I want to make something of my life.
I know that I don't want to drift.
I know that I don't trust myself
to sift the good from the bad, the better from the best;
I know that I don't want to spend my time
constantly checking the map, and wondering what I have missed,
and getting nowhere.

And Jesus looked at me again, and I knew he saw
everything: my trembling faith, my all-too-human hesitation
my longing to be – whatever I was supposed to be;
and he said again, 'You – follow me!'

Just a minute, Lord!
I took off my watch,
and I found my diary stroke personal organiser
and I handed them over.
Lord, my times are in your hands:
as from *now*
I will follow you
sure I will.

PROPER 9

Gardeners' Question Time

Galatians 6:(1-6), 7-16; Luke 10:1-11, 16-20

One, two, three and five make eight:
a sum is the total of its parts.
So is the sum of my life the total of its parts:
(only the grace of God can change the slate).

Every day, every minute, I am sowing,
every thought, every choice, every word
is adding up, growing me a harvest, now
or later: will it be a rich reward
or a burning of barren stubble?

Perhaps it's sentimental to say
that we're nearer God's heart in a garden
than anywhere else on earth,
but I do envy gardeners their rich insight
into the process of seedtime and harvest:
the planning made possible only because of predictability,
that what is sown is what will appear;
the preparation, quality of seed, and patient waiting.
Fail to clear the rubble, sow corrupt seed
or let the wind deliver what it will –
then I must not be surprised
to reap thorns and thistles, trouble and whirlwind.

Let me then ask these gardeners,
and the great Gardener,
how can I sow and reap to please the Spirit?

Sow, first, the good seed of the Word of God
(refusing to modify it, genetically or otherwise
to make it palatable to a picky generation);

broadcast it with generosity and love
first in my own life, then in every life that touches mine.
Plant in peace seeds of healing
and of reconciliation,
seeds of a new kingdom, a new way of being,
promising shoots of hope
and fruits of right good living,

and if the Word is not welcomed, do not despair:
the next field, or the next season
will yet yield a harvest.

Next, sow the good seed of thought and action
brought under the searchlight of Christ;
If physically I am what I eat
then spiritually I am what I think and do
in relation to God,
above, beside and within me.

Is my mind like a marketplace
where peddlers of any philosophy can set their stall?
A free-for-all, where the loudest voice,
the largest headline, the line of least resistance
dictate my choice?
Or do I allow my thoughts to be sifted,
wheat from chaff, and consign to the four winds
what cannot nourish,
what may even steal my soul's food?

Right action follows only from right thought
though there is many a distraction
between the one and the other;
what I *really* think will be conveyed (betrayed?)
by what I actually get round to *doing*.
And what I *do* confirms, implants that thought
and germinates another
and so the fruit begins to grow:
thought – action – habit – character – destiny.

And if my spiritual growth seems slow and stunted, do not despair:
allow the Gardener to prune
and there *will* be a harvest.

Then there's the sowing of good deeds,
good seeds, first in the family field
then on the open, common land.

Seeds sown not to produce the showiest flowers,
the largest veg for the competition,
the longest lasting, sweetest smelling, tallest growing,
look at me I'm wonderful and *now* will you come to church?
Rather seeds sown in the dark,
quietly, patiently, persistently:
trees for shelter, herbs for healing,
flowers, white for peace, blue for remembrance,
red and gold for joy;
apples for teacher,
strawberries, cherries and plums
to colour and sweeten the day.

And if those deeds go unremarked, do not despair:
God receives all that is given
and weaves it for good.

Seedtime and harvest,
God's promise to Noah, and all mankind,
for ever: physically, to provide;
spiritually, to work out our own salvation
in fear and trembling.

Looking now at my own garden
pulls me up short:
I manage to keep the grass cut, and gouge out
the worst of the dandelions
so at a quick glance, maybe
it doesn't look *too* bad –
but there's ivy and nettles and creeping bindweed
and next door's cat has peed on the sweet pea shoots

and that horrible bush that doesn't even flower
has taken over again, and nothing will grow
in the corner bed because it's full of old tree roots
and the fence is falling down –

Lord, did you have to plant this analogy
right on my doorstep?
There's so much work to be done . . .

PROPER 10

Simply Divine

Deuteronomy 30:9-14; Psalm 25:1-10; Colossians 1:1-14; Luke 10:25-37

If you ask me,
the mark of a truly great thinker
is that they can say it in words of one syllable.

I mean,
if it's that complicated,
it can't be that important, can it?
Because large swathes of the population,
including me,
would never understand
and that wouldn't be fair – would it?

Well, it's a wonderful excuse
for ignoring Wittgenstein
and whole shelves full of theologians and philosophers
who don't seem to know
when they've stopped making any sort of sense
and disappeared up their –
I mean, down a blind alley.

Seriously, though –
Confucius limited himself
to relatively few well-chosen words;
Jesus, it seems, wrote nothing,
taught in parables, and praised God
that he had hidden his truth
from the so-called wise and intelligent,
spurned their learned paragraphs,
and communicated it to children,
illustrated, even.

Not that his truth is not profound beyond reckoning:
water of life
deep enough to drown a mammoth
but lapping low enough for a little mouse to drink safely;
and that is enough
for most of us,

that is enough:
because, as the man said,
it's not what we *don't* understand that bothers us
(or should bother us)
but what we *do* understand –
and choose to ignore.

Like Moses told the Israelites,
it's not that hard to get your head round what God says
but to put your heart into it:
go on, just *do* it!

Like David wrote in his psalm,
you don't need a degree to fathom God's decree
but a humble, obedient spirit:
go on, just *do* it!

Like Jesus said to the expert in law,
it's not an understanding of the finer points that you lack
but the love to live it:
go on, just *do* it!

Like Paul wrote to the church at Colossae,
it's not that you've only been told the half –
just that you haven't grasped the fullness of life in Christ:
go on, just *do* it!

Knowledge,
little or great,
can be a dangerous thing,
insatiable, puffing up, pleased with itself;
putting letters after my name,

pennies, maybe, in my pocket: useless, though
when it comes to writing that name in the Book of Life
or storing up treasure in heaven . . .

When it comes to that final examination
I think it will not be academic
but vocational;
not 'How much do you know?
Tell me about the minor prophets,
Thomas Aquinas and Revelation'
but 'What have you *done* with what you know?
Did you go and tell your friend
that Jesus is sensational?'

We should not disconnect our brains, though,
neglect to use God-given reason,
refuse to venture into that deep water;
all that God has given,
animal, vegetable, mineral,
abstract, even
invites the scientist to search, and sift, and speculate:
but only as a spur
to wonder, worship and translate
new understanding into new living.

Philosophy and science –
love of wisdom and of knowledge –
like so many things, make good servants
but bad masters;
ask always 'Whom do you serve?
Do you illuminate
or darken the counsel of God with so many words?'

For most of us, perhaps,
mystery is essential
to our grasp of God;
fullness of comprehension
lies, if anywhere, in heaven: and that is good.
Meanwhile, Jesus is all-sufficient:

pardoning and guarding what is past,
guiding and providing for the present,
promising to all who follow with persistence,
patience, reverence, obedience,
a perfect future.

Deep down
our need is not to understand
all
but,
simply,
to know the next step
and the one who takes our hand.

PROPER 11

Contract Catering

Amos 8:1-12; Luke 10:38-42

Remember that classic epitaph:
'Erected by her sorrowing brothers
in memory of Martha Clay:
Here lies one who lived for others;
now she has peace. And so have they.'

Strange that she should be another Martha: what's in a name?
Martha, Mary and Lazarus.
I bet they were both the older sister too, the one who
made sure their necks and their handkerchiefs were clean,
organised the packed lunches and checked the loo rolls,
rationed out the cake and plasticine.

'But what's so bad about that?'
we murmur under our breath;
all right, so we're supposed to be rooting for Mary,
artistically posed, as ever, at the feet of Jesus –
we know that,
but secretly
we're on your side, Martha, we're with you all the way!

Why, every time we meet you
it's there, in the kitchen, with your servant's apron,
slaving over a hot stove, counting plates, putting the finishing touches
to the soufflé:
Martha's contract catering, weddings and funerals a speciality;
other functions by arrangement.
No party too large or too small;

make no mistake,
she's a real gem
hospitality queen

a godsend
and Jesus *loved* her, just the way she was, apron and all;

Martha and her contract catering, weddings and funerals a speciality
other functions by arrangement
no party too large or too small;
personal attention guaranteed.

Or was it?

Or was that – the personal attention – the gift of letting someone know they *matter* – the one thing that was missing?

The danger, of course, is that we fall,
we Marthas, into the trap
of missing the wood for the trees,
of mistaking the means for the end.
We worry that the cream teas will run out of cream
and fail to see that lady who always comes, and eats
like she hasn't eaten for a week:
at least,
we see her, but we do not really take her in.
We pride ourselves that all the vegetables are home grown
and fail to pick up that John, the widower,
is the only one who has come alone.

Martha, you are distracted by many things,
you have quality standards to keep up,
a reputation to maintain;
next year you're going for Charter Mark
and they'll come and assess the durability of your toothpicks,
and whether they come from protected rainforest timber.

But Martha,
it's not the doing things right that matters, my dear,
but doing the right things.

Did you know
that even after this feast, this Martha special,

this Delia Smith, Jamie Oliver, Rick Stein masterpiece
these people will go to bed hungry – ?

Hungry, Lord?

Hungry. There is famine in this land.

Lord, with respect, when did you last go to Tesco's?
Perhaps you're confusing us with Sudan.

No. Your famine is worse – yes, worse,
a curse of this age, and this place;
it is a famine of hearing the word of God.

But Lord, I am too busy.
Yes, Martha, you are too busy,
he, she and it are too busy,
we are too busy, all of you are too busy, the whole darned world is too busy;
if you are too busy to take time
to listen
and hear the word of God:
for that is the one thing that is needed.

Martha,
you are hot and bothered,
you are frustrated because there is so much to do.
You are driven
by the tyranny of the urgent.
But how do you know if it is also important?
How do you know it all *needs* doing – *really* needs doing –
if you haven't let me whisper in your ear
and show you how *I* see it all?
Even I, your Lord, have left many things undone,
many sick still suffering, many people untaught,
many storms not stilled, many battles not fought:
even for God's Son there could never be quite enough
hours in the day, enough days in the week, enough weeks in the year;
and so

I did only what I saw my Father doing
and slipped away alone, night or early morning,
knelt at his feet, to hear
what that might be . . .

and it was enough. In fact, it was just right.

Martha,
I love you,
I love your heart that longs to give, to fill the hungry with good things;
but remember there is a hunger not satisfied by bread
(or even by chocolate),
hunger that's masked by plenty,
hunger that *should* remain
sharp, urgent, pleading;
hunger for truth, for meaning, for love – for God:
soul hunger.
To be sure, the body needs feeding but, however well fed, it dies:
the wise hunger
for soul food, for
the soul, fed on the bread of life, will live for ever.
And *I am*
the bread of life.

Come,
you Marthas,
you who labour and are heavy laden,
put down that tray:
kneel at my feet
and listen . . .

PROPER 12

A Moving Experience

Genesis 18:20-32; Luke 11:1-13

So often you hear people say
'We can do nothing, only pray . . .'
Only pray? How little we know
of the momentous amount of activity,
the critical mass of energy
that is true intercession:

moving, and being moved.

Moving the cavity insulation from my heart's walls
to allow me to feel the gravity of the situation beyond;
moving me into that pregnant place between seeking Lord
and lost world to plead, for each with the other;
moving mountains of apathy, fear and unbelief;
moving the very willing heart of God himself.

If intercession is then the daily work-out
for those who would aim to be spiritually fit,
Abraham is, perhaps, our first personal trainer –
surely a champion of lost causes, if ever there was one
(Sodom and Gomorrah? I ask you!
Even for a seasoned campaigner).
From Abraham learn that, whilst God cannot deny himself,
such is his management style there is no situation
beyond disputation, or even reprieve,
if we care enough;

but sometimes, I believe
God waits in the wings,
waits for an Abraham with the temerity, with the compassion
to agonise and argue the severity of the plan,
with passion enough for the Lord's reputation

to challenge him: will not the judge of the earth do right?
God waits in the wings
for an Abraham to care enough.
For me to care enough.

Why? To add power to his elbow?
Of course not: his arm is neither too short nor too weak to save.
Why then? Surely to grow Christ-likeness in him who prays,
build spiritual muscle,
heart muscle,
flexed for those next mountains that need to be moved.

Abraham dared, then, to engage with God
with a respectful stubbornness that won from his God
a concession: though there were not
ten righteous people (for no one is righteous, no, not one;
God cannot discard his holiness, and so
the cities were destroyed): yet
for Abraham's sake his family was spared,
a reluctant lot,
but trophies of intercession.

Abraham, intercessor:
moving and being moved,
moved into that pregnant place between holy God
and unholy city to plead, for each with the other.

Moved like Moses to care enough
for his careless, faithless people:
'Forgive their sin, Lord – but if not,
blot me out of the book you have written!'
Surely no man has greater love than this,
willing to lay down his life for his friends;
surely Moses cared enough?
But though he stood to reason with God,
neither was his the righteousness which sufficed
to set his people completely free.

Moses, intercessor:
moving and being moved,
moved into that pregnant place between faithful God
and promiscuous people to plead, for each with the other.

Moved like the suffering servant
and son of God, Jesus Christ,
tempted as we are, yet without sin: who cared enough
to pour out his life's blood, sufficient sacrifice
for the whole unrighteous world
and yes!
Moving mountains of alienation and debt;
moving the very willing heart of God himself.

Jesus, intercessor:
moving and being moved,
moved into that pregnant place between seeking Father
and prodigal sons to plead, for each with the other.

Jesus, who teaches us now to pray
like the friend at midnight:
or rather, not like the friend at midnight –
Knock knock!
Who's there?
Your friend.
It's midnight!
I know, that's the whole point, the shops are shut.
Give over, I'm asleep.
Oh, go on – I'm your friend, remember?
There are friends and there are confounded nuisances –
and so on,
until he finally staggers up, with half a stale loaf and a very bad grace.

No, when we come to our father God,
it is to a true friend.
Knock knock!
Who's there?
A friend of your Son.
Welcome . . . what can I do for you?

You know he taught us to pray, give us this *day* our daily bread –
Yes?
Does that apply to night time too?
Of course: whatever you need, whenever you need it,

only ask, and you will receive
(not always the thing you asked for, but you *will* always
receive an answer);
only seek, and you will find
(not always the thing you thought you were seeking, but you *will* always
find the wisdom of God);
only knock, and the door will be opened
(not always the door to health, wealth and instant happiness, but
always the door to the kingdom of heaven).

Only pray?
Only pray, care enough, intercessor,
to wrestle, plead, engage, struggle, debate,
argue, agonise, remonstrate, weep:

moving and being moved,
moved into that pregnant place between seeking Lord
and lost world to plead, for each with the other.

Hear the voice of men
and feel your heart moved;
hear the voice of God
and see mountains moved.

PROPER 13

Two Teachers Take Time Out To Talk

Ecclesiastes 1:2, 12-14, 2:18-23; Luke 12:13-21

J Well, Solomon, I read your book again the other day;
it's brilliant – and infuriating; perceptive,
and potentially dangerous. I don't know
whether to love it or hate it!

S I could well say the same about yours.

J The biographies, you mean? I never wrote anything.

S Wise man. Mind you, I never wrote half of mine:
you know how they will put words in your mouth. Having said that,
it's a pretty fair record of how I felt about
this whole pointless exercise you call life.

J There you go! That's what's so infuriating: you're such
a plaguey pessimist – you, of all people, who enjoyed
such power, such privilege, so many possessions,
passions, palaces, popularity even: you were granted so much,
but counted it nothing.

S All right, so I'm an ungrateful wretch! But that's my point,
exactly: I had everything the world could offer, everything
that money could buy; been there, seen it,
got the T-shirt to prove it. You could say I created
paradise on earth – and I found myself sated,
but not satisfied.

J Why?

S Exactly. I couldn't answer that question: *Why*?
What was it all *for*?

J And so you hated your life. Was it that frustrating,
not to know why?

S You know it was. And you know why – come on,
it was you who told the story of the farmer, who needed
bigger barns for all his wealth: but what was the point?
That very night, he died.

J That's right.

S Well, that's it, isn't it? Death, the infernal jester,
death, the uninvited guest, death, the great leveller:
death mocks our certainties, rocks our securities,
knocks at my door and separates me from mine . . .

J Ah, now that's where I'd disagree.

S Pardon? I thought we were saying the same thing –
why work for what you can't keep, for what
at any minute may be snatched away:
why seek knowledge that fails to comprehend
the real mysteries? Why play power games, or fight
the law of pleasure's diminishing returns?
Always death interrupts and has the final say.

J You speak of death as 'separating me and mine':
I disagree. None of these things is yours; therein
lies the rub – and the hope.

S I never did find it easy to follow your drift, you
with your parables and paradoxes: give me proverbs, any day!
And I must catch up on a thousand years – though I must say,
I see no change in human nature: *there's* the rub.
I see no end to chasing after wind, no hope.

J I repeat, I disagree! Listen, now:
What if – the wealth of the world were not simply *there*
to be raided or traded, paraded, bought or fought for –
but was God's to lend, for a time, a short time only

to see how we would tend it, send it, spend it;
how will you craft your life, and the life of your friend?

S No matter: whatever I make of life,
death will come and make an end.

J Listen now:
what if . . . there is not only life before death
but life *after* death?

S Prove it!

J I did – but we'll come to that later.
If death *is* the end, then sure: it's hard to make sense
of anything much – morality, love, the need for sense;
eat, drink and be merry is as good a maxim as any,
if tomorrow we die.
But if we die to one world only in order to enter another –
what then? If we leave what was only ever intended
to be left –

S If, if – what kind of fairy tale might that be? Do you see me
as some kind of child needing a happy ending?

J I see you as a teacher too honest to embrace humanism,
too ethical to embrace hedonism,
too perceptive to embrace pragmatism –
and downright depressing.

S Thanks.

J You paint a true picture of life without God, but I fear
it will pave the way for the suicide bomber just as much
as the picture of life *after* death being all that matters;
in both, life is cheap
and that is a travesty of justice,
a lie of the devil, and a slur
on the character of God.

S Strong words.

J I know something of the joy, and the anticipation of joy
in the heart of God,
delight and excitement in the creation
of every good and perfect gift, of life itself –
for you
to enjoy, but *not* to have or to hold:
rather, to give you a foretaste of what he is like,
of what is to come for you who know how to hold
lightly, with reverence and appreciation,
and to let go without hesitation or regret
when the time comes.

S When *death* comes. Like I said – that much is certain:
the rest is speculation.

J No, the rest is trust.
Trust me, Solomon – I've been there, seen it, got the scars
to prove it. Death *will* come but will no longer have the last word;
no longer make an end of it:
he is the pretender to the throne, and I
have trampled him under my feet as I walked free
from the grave to claim my kingdom.
Will you come too? Will you trust me?

S Perhaps – perhaps I will dare to believe
vanity is vain, futility futile; instead
of chasing after the wind, what if I were to allow
that wind to blow where it will, to blow me
where it will: even into your kingdom?
Would that be the final wisdom?

PROPER 14

Tracing the Family

Genesis 15:1-6; Hebrews 11:1-3, 8-16

I used to dream
what it would be like to have chocolate cake in my lunch box every day,
to understand those division sums without even having to try,
to kiss the girl with the green ribbons,
but I had to learn that life's not like that;
healthy eating is all the rage,
I am not a natural mathematician
and she hit me;
and I went back to my mum that night
and let her read me a story.

I used to dream
what it would be like to be an airline pilot with the whole sky at my fingertips,
to be the lead singer – no, the drummer – with the boy band,
to get into the basketball team,
but I had to learn that life's not like that;
you need maths and physics, or a lot of money,
the right image, and a lot of luck
and be six foot three;
that night my granddad told me about
his seventy years on the sheep farm.

I used to dream
what it would be like to have a job with a BMW and shares thrown in,
to earn enough money to buy a place in the Mediterranean sun,
to have four perfect children,
but I had to learn that life's not like that;
it means the stress of the city and a sixty hour week,
Italian lessons with Silvio at night school
and – perfect kids??

My great-grandmother saw the first cars appear
but never went more than ten miles from home.

Not, of course, that my life has been too bad
and who ever promised that it should be more?
But it's hard to be one of those creatures who dreams
yet does not know what dreams are for.

As one by one they pass their sell-by date
unrealised, I cease to look ahead
to find myself, define myself by what will be
and turn to look behind instead,

asking, 'Whose child am I?'

The second favourite reason why we go online, it seems,
is genealogy;
unsure where I'm heading, as dreams fade
I need at least to know where I come from,
that somewhere I am held, somewhere I belong:
in all this vast space with too much freedom,
and too little,

tell me I am somebody's child.

And there's the miracle!
As I go back, and back, make my way back along the branches,
back down the trunk, down, down to the ground
and dig away at the very roots of my tree
there I find him,
my first father,
the father who thought that he would never have children:
Abraham
whose children now outnumber the stars in the sky
or the grains of sand on the seashore
and all because he would not let go of his dream
but challenged God, saying, 'You promised! You promised me
a child – don't fob me off now with talk of any other reward!'
And God saw his stubborn faith, and knew he had found the right man
and performed his promised miracle –

twenty-five years later, mind,
twenty-five years! But Abraham hung in there,
faint, at times, but pursuing the God of promise
and the promise of God,
willing to be part of that promise that was so much greater
than his comprehending, that stretched a million miles beyond his seeing
and a million years beyond his earthly living;
willing to trust God that later, who knows how much later?
would come the blessing, the happy ending
which could never, quite, have happened without him.

And am I a child of my father?

Going, without knowing where,
doing, without knowing why,
hoping, without knowing when
yet trusting, trusting that God cannot lie

and one day he will stoop down, make a paste with clay,
anoint my eyes, and I will see
in a flash the whole picture, see that I am a star in the sky,
a grain of sand on the shore, and that without me
that happy ending could never, quite, have happened.

Abraham, when I look at you
I begin to understand how some peoples worship their ancestors!
As a dad, you take some beating:
fearing God, yet straight-talking;
ready always to take him at his word – hold him to it,
and be held by it – which is faith.
Such faith inspires hope
prompts obedience
counters disappointment
disarms fear
builds endurance
and sows seeds of joy.

No, I shall not worship you
but I am so glad to have found you,

found that you are my father, and I, too, am on the receiving end
of the promises of God –
not, as I so often think, on the receiving end
of the demands of the law: even a life where every dream came true
would fall at this hurdle. No,
I am not a child of Moses
but of Abraham, thank God:

Abraham
who is still hanging in there,
bless him, waiting to receive every last mouthful
of the promises of God,
waiting till all the family has been traced
and blessed,
all who believe the promise of God
that there *is* something worth waiting for
falling for, getting up again for, laughing, crying,
living, dreaming, dying for.
Abraham
waiting still for those long-time-coming children,
including me.

Whose child am I?
A child of Abraham
and of God

and that is a dream
that will prove to be no dream,
but the most real, and most blessed thing
about me.

PROPER 15

But What about Health and Safety?

Jeremiah 23:23-29; Hebrews 11:29–12:2; Luke 12:49-56

It's just as well Jesus didn't have the Health and Safety Executive
to contend with, or the whole Christianity thing would never
have got off the starting blocks.

As it was,
he seems to have inherited his Father's apparent lack of concern
for his employees' worldly well-being:
mocked, persecuted, flogged?
Stoned, imprisoned, murdered in cold blood?
Walking the world as a refugee, down-and-out, 'gentleman' of the road?
All in a day's work.

OK, the long-term benefits are to die for: but the job description
and current working conditions are not for the faint-hearted.

Company Mission Statement:
to set the earth on fire
(or, in a later assessment, to turn the world upside down).

Objectives:
to give priority to those who have no economic pulling power,
and no voice;
to dispense justice at all levels;
to bring the world's kingdoms under the kingship of God.

Aims:
to lose weight: anything that makes us too slow, or
too comfortable must go;
to speak the word of God faithfully: the truth, the whole
truth and nothing but the truth;
to get our hands dirty;
to meet opposition with perseverance and humility.

All employees should make themselves available 24/7,
and undertake whatever tasks their line manager may ask them to do
(nothing there about 'reasonably').

Training and equipment will be provided.

No claims for damages or compensation for loss of health, goods or life will be considered under any circumstances.

Perhaps if we were a bit more honest with our advertising,
our churches wouldn't be so exclusively full of little old ladies.
Not that there's anything wrong with little old ladies:
we'd be surprised what many of them got up to in their prime –
and many an arthritic knee is the result of many a long hour of prayer.
But when the only challenge given to most Christians
is to keep awake during the sermon, what can you expect?
In this race, this relay race, it's a blazing torch
we should be handing on, not a raffle ticket.
God is not just cosy – encouraging those who stay at home and knit;
he is also the Lord of heaven's armies, looking for those
who will volunteer for the front line. Tell it like it is (see above),
substitute boot camp for home group, and maybe
we'll begin to win the real men (of both sexes) . . .

We are dazzled today by so many stars and superstars:
but where are those real men,
the heroes – martyrs even – of whom our present world is not worthy?

Blessed are the peacemakers: but blessed, too, are the arsonists.
Blessed are those whose soft answer turns away wrath:
    but blessed, too, are the prophets who stir it all up.
Blessed are the meek, whose strength is submitted:
    but blessed, too, are those who march in,
    all guns blazing, to fight for the powerless.
Blessed are those who keep their hands clean:
    but blessed, too, are those who get them dirty
    for the sake of the gospel.
Blessed are those who care for the sick and needy:
    but blessed, too, are those who do not consider their health

too high a price to pay for the spiritual health of another.
Blessed are those who rescue the captives:
but blessed, too, are those who do not consider their safety
too high a price to pay for the final safety of the other in the arms of God.

Health and safety! What a mixed blessing . . .
when sense degenerates into smothering, reasonable attention
into the addition of so many Pharisaical jots and tittles that any action other than breathing is rendered inadvisable, and life is reduced to existence . . .
then we must pray for a people prepared to throw caution to the wind,
for greater things are at stake.

O Lord most high,
pour out your Spirit again here, today:
may our sons and our daughters prophesy,
hearing your clear call to live dangerously;
may our young men see visions
of challenges issued, battles joined, and won;
may our old men dream dreams
of the end of the age, your kingdom come, your will done.

Spirit, pull that soft carpet from under our feet,
give us our boots and our marching orders;
remind us that truly serving Christ will challenge the highest flyer,
the bravest soldier, the greatest idealist, the hungriest adventurer:
challenge, and satisfy
all who will dare to live for him
without reservation.

PROPER 16

Bringing It All Back Home

Isaiah 58:9b-14

Drop the debt
Feed the hungry
Free the oppressed
Save the children
Make poverty history
World Aids Day!

Tick the box
Join the protest
Write the letter
Wear the ribbon
Buy the T-shirt
Sign the cheque

and feel,
with just the smallest hint of smugness,
that I've done my bit?

I fear
that it's all too easy,
too easy to hide my casual concern
behind those big headlines from faraway places
which, after all, I cannot visit, nor fully imagine;
yes, I will drink the fair trade coffee;
yes, I will put a pound in the box;
yes, I will try to remember them when I'm praying –
what more can I do
to lift their yoke of oppression?

I'm about to let myself off the hook
when I hear the voice of the Lord, saying
something about 'bringing it all back home'

reminding me there is more than one way to be oppressed,
and have I addressed
or even acknowledged
the need on my own patch?

Isn't my father-in-law oppressed
by his failing health and the rising damp in the walls?
Could someone take him out for a drink,
to talk of old times? Could someone speak to his landlord,
take the firm line he no longer dares?
Could I? Will I?

Isn't my boss oppressed
by the gossips and critics who lack understanding
and time to help, but have plenty of time to undermine?
Could someone deflect the poisoned arrows,
point out the damage, propose a new way of working?
Could I? Will I?

Isn't the family down the road oppressed
by lack of space, and time, and money:
all the demands of a growing family?
Could someone take the kids for a day,
share shopping trips, cheap cooking tips?
Could I? Will I?

Thinking globally has that hint of glamour
but perhaps my lessons in charity
need to begin at home.

I like to think I can help *rebuild*
the ruins where earthquakes have struck:
spend a little time
to read the news, and pray, and maybe
spend a little money.

But maybe God is thinking I can help rebuild
the ruins where the earthquake of sudden death has struck
my neighbour:

spend some time (not a little)
to be there, listen, make tea, whatever it takes
to rebuild a life.
Spend – myself.

I like to think I can help *repair*
the broken walls where the hurricane smashed the sea defences:
spend a little time
to read the news, and pray, and maybe
spend a little money.

But maybe God is thinking I can help repair
the broken walls where rising interest rates, redundancy
and debt have smashed my friend's security:
spend some time (not a little)
to be there, listen, find wise advice, whatever it takes
to repair a life.
Spend – myself.

I like to think I can help *restore*
streets with dwellings where war leaves rubble and refugees:
spend a little time
to read the news, and pray, and maybe
spend a little money.

But maybe God is thinking I can help restore
the streets with dwellings where desertion and divorce
leave anger, brokenness and guilt:
spend some time (not a little)
to be there, to listen, to speak healing, whatever it takes
to restore a home.
Spend – myself.

Rebuilding, repairing, restoring
God's construction workers
here, and there, and everywhere.

In Asia, where I stayed, there was much
rebuilding, repairing and restoring

going on – day and night, it seemed;
workers would come and live on site,
work whenever,
not 9 to 5, or 8 to 6
but whenever there was a job to be done.
Work and leisure merged in a lifestyle of
construction.

So God calls his construction team,
not for a 'quick-fix' visit,
not for a statutory day's work
but to come and live on site,
work whenever,
whenever there is a job to be done;
work and leisure merged in a lifestyle of
service to him, of
construction:

first learn my charity at home,
looking to lift these local yokes of oppression
hands on;
then come to respond, if I will, to those wider issues,
not with a gesture,
but with love and humility born of involving myself
in the waste of the world
and my own part in it.

PROPER 17

Make Way for Angels

Psalm 112; Hebrews 13:1-8, 15, 16; Luke 14:1, 7-14

I suspect
that when my life is too full of *stuff*
there is no room for angels
and that's a pity.

I can be so concerned
with closing loopholes,
providing for contingencies,
making sure there's enough in the kitty
for rainy days and possible tuition fees
that it seems I have no need
for angels;

of course, you could call this
sensible, responsible – and so it is.
But I sometimes wonder
if it is *altogether* godly:
whether, sometimes, God would prefer
to send us angels,
surprise us with miracles?

Remember that great missionary to China,
Hudson Taylor –
faced with a friend in great need,
but down to his last half crown.
If only – if only he had *two* coins, instead of just the one,
how gladly he'd have given his friend a share!
In China, though, he knew he must depend
on God alone to care for him; was this to be the test?
And so he wrestled, as did Jesus, with temptation
and won through;

giving his friend all,
he knew the comfort of angels,
confirmation of his call
and God, Jehovah Jireh, the Lord who provides.

To give gladly,
cheerfully, hilariously, even!
To give and not to count the cost,
nor look for any reward.
To give not from the pocket
but from the heart.
How many doors are unlocked,
how many angels released from heaven!
Like a crazy man
in a black and white 20s film
dancing wildly down the street,
swinging round the lamppost
singing, singing in the rain
'I've got nothing, I've got nothing,
and nothing's got hold of me . . .'

Free . . .
Free, at last,
from too much carefulness; free
from that lingering love of Mammon; free
to be led by angels,
to be fed by angels.

Manna, after all, does not grow on trees
but in the wilderness.

But is such generosity,
such disinterested goodness,
possible? Are we ever free, you ask,
from mixed motives, hidden agendas?
Are we not now tempted
to give extravagantly
simply so that God may send us angels?
To put him to the test?

To add to our spiritual experience?
To update our testimony?
Always pride lurks around the next corner.

But this, too, may be a trap
if it endangers our obedience
to the command to give hilariously,
entertain strangers gregariously,
care for ourselves precariously
but love our brother from the heart;
for only as we seek this generous living
does it really dawn on us
that our hearts are deceitful, and mean:
that we lack the gaiety and grace
to give all,
knowing you can send a thousand angels,
but even if you don't –

I will do it
because I am reborn:
because you have put a new heart in me,
your heart
and I can do no other.

Only then
will I entertain strangers,
not because they may be angels
but because you want to make every stranger your friend
and may need to do it through me;

only then
will I cast my bread upon the waters
not so that it may return to me later
but because you have fish out there who are hungry
and may need to feed them through me;

only then
will I sell all I have and give to the poor
not because I will have my reward in heaven

but because both they, and I, need to know
that you are the Lord who provides.

God's good gifts are surely meant
to be kept in circulation:
life blood, without which the body will die.
Today, I am able to give to you,
trusting God that tomorrow
you will be willing to give to me;
and so a greater good is growing:
our relationship
of faith, and hope and love
for God and each other.
You may be called to be an angel to me
and who knows?
I may even be called to be an angel to you
and so
we, who were made that little bit lower than angels
grow
(and if, in amongst all this,
God chooses to send us the real thing,
I shan't say no!).

PROPER 18

Left, Right and Centre

Deuteronomy 30:15-20; Psalm 1; Luke 14:25-33

Left, right or centre:
why is it that I always choose
the slowest
of the traffic lanes, or checkout queues?

The outside lane,
all Audis and white vans
was moving along nicely: until it ground to a halt
and all the HGVs and 2CVs surged past on my left.

The middle queue
of trolleys was shortest; how was I to know the one in front
had faulty goods, the one in front of her
a dodgy credit card?

Left, right or centre?
By nature most of us, I guess,
are likely not to be extremist;
being reasonable people who have learned
to see both sides of any question, we'd prefer
to choose the centre.
Unfortunately,
according to Moses,
the Psalmist,
Jesus, and ultimately
God,
there is no middle way.

And choose we must.
Choice will not always be the privilege
that politicians claim;

it is, though, the mark of man
created from the dust, yes,
but also in the image of God: free to choose
his character and destiny.
Life or death? Blessing or curse? Upright or scoffer?
Well, it's obvious, isn't it?
Who, in their right mind, would choose death and destruction
when blessing and life are on offer?

But what was that about a broad road to destruction,
a narrow pathway to eternal life?
In practice, it just ain't that easy . . .

Do you remember
in those cheap and cheerful children's puzzle books
the page that looked like tangled string –
six ends, six threads: five led
to doom and destruction,
only one to the sparkly treasure.
Of course I knew I wanted the treasure –
but which of the strings to choose?
And it would never be the one
that looked most likely.

Moses spoke to a nation who,
having chosen wrongly,
lost an entire generation in the wilderness.
Jesus spoke to a great multitude, of whom
one would suppose, less rather than more
would end up squeezing through that narrow door.
The right road can appear horribly wrong,
hardly a blessing in sight
while the wrong road seems sunny, and fun
and beguilingly right

and much of the time the road just seems –
indeterminate: neither right, nor wrong
just grey, and sort of OK

and it's hard to grasp
that all the world's millions
with their billions of assorted choices,
good and bad (but never indifferent?)
are bound, inexorably,
for one of *only two* destinations . . .
And in the end
it will depend
not on the balance of those choices, good and bad
but on which road they travel,
which string they hold in their hand.

'Choose life!
Put your eggs in the Moses basket:
love God, listen to him, walk in his way
and you will have blessings,
blessings of long life in a settled land
but if not, displacement and death.'
Well, what else could I say?

But was it inevitable, then as now
that although the spirit is willing,
willing me to choose life,
the flesh is weak,
too weak to put my feet in the footprints of God
as the path narrows and grows steep?
Hinds' feet in high places?
No thanks: I don't have a head for heights;
I think I'll lie low,
go with the flow,
find a way round this mountain
with all its demands.

Not so;
Jesus said there was only one way
and he never said it would be easy.
'Don't start,' he said 'unless you intend to finish;
count the cost. How much do you want life,
real life, eternal life?

Look at me . . .
Do you trust me that I alone know the road,
that I alone have travelled it?
That it's impossibly steep, impassably high
and the only way you can master it
is to let me carry you?
Look at me . . .
If you see my claims as absurd,
my promise as empty,
my offer an insult to your pride,
my route restrictive and irksome –
well, you have the choice, left or right,
broad or narrow:

but there is
no middle way.'

Left, right – but no centre?
Lord!
Help me, this time, to choose well:
to be born again and laid,
this time, not in the Moses basket
but in your arms.

PROPER 19

Carpenter's Rule, OK?

Psalm 51:1-10; 1 Timothy 1:12-17; Luke 15:1-10

What's normal?

Not so long ago, pasta and pizza
were foreign concepts;
a slow cooker was an ancient Aga
and we only ate fruit and veg in season.

What's normal?

Not so long ago, children called the teacher
'Sir' and sat in rows
and a mouse
would never have been allowed in the classroom.

What's normal?

Not so long ago, beauty was reckoned
in terms of health,
child-bearing hips
and a pretty turn of the ankle.

What's normal?

It all depends on what we're told,
the magazines we read,
the company we keep, the packages we're sold,
the rapidly receding boundaries
of reality TV;
I mean,
if they can do it on *EastEnders,* and
celebrities go through it in the jungle,
if we've seen it on *Big Brother*

and it's been exposed on Jerry Springer,
if politicians say it on the chat-shows
and housewives play it for a pastime –
it must be normal, right?

And because it's normal, it must be
OK,
right?

That's what we have to tell ourselves, isn't it?
That what *is*
is normal
and what's normal
is OK
or we'd all go mad with uncertainty
and guilt – wouldn't we?

But, you know what –
sometimes it pays to be a sad crossword addict,
nose in dictionary,
for there are gems to be found,
happy etymological accidents.

NORM can be 'an average level of achievement'
guess we're all happy with that;
or it can be 'a standard that is required as normal'
ah, rough ground there;
but more! *Norm* is from the Latin *norma*
meaning 'a carpenter's rule, or square'
and *normal* means conforming to
that rule:
now there's a cause
to pause for thought . . .

What's normal?

It all depends on what we're told
and if we trust the storyteller.
According to a certain – I would say

trustworthy – carpenter, correction!
our 'normal' is not at all OK.
His rule requires quite a different standard,
even God's gold standard of perfection
and all who fall short, who are merely 'normal',
we would say, 'only human'
are – *sinners*?

But surely he can't blame us for being only human –
that's how we were born, for heaven's sake!
Exactly. 'Surely I was sinful at birth,
sinful from the time my mother conceived me.'
What, before I'd even opened my mouth to cry?
Yes, you were a 'normal' human being
in proud possession of a sinful nature,
incapable of measuring up
to the carpenter's rule.

Unfair?
Perhaps, but that's how it is. Heaven and earth may pass away
but the carpenter's rule is constant
and that's how it is:
but before you turn your back and flounce off in disgust
wait! and learn of the other unfairness:

It is *sinners* who are special,
it is *sinners* who gather round Jesus,
who find themselves his preferred company; he came
especially for sinners,
sinners who will believe him
that they were made for more than mere 'normality';
it is sinners who bring joy to the angels in heaven
when they own that name,
finding it to be the word
that brings the shepherd running,
the woman hurrying to light her lamp and search for them.

Only sinners can be found
only sinners can be forgiven

only sinners can be freed
only sinners can be friends of God.

Unfair?
Perhaps, but that's how it is. Heaven and earth may pass away
but the carpenter's rule is constant
and that's how it is.

And we are so suggestible, susceptible –
accepting the skinny supermodels telling us
we're three sizes too big,
the advertisers selling us
a cooler car, a hotter holiday, cosmetic surgery
if we're to be acceptable.
In the face of which an army of psychiatrists and counsellors
struggle to teach us how to love ourselves –

but we refuse to listen to the one who *knows*
we *are* beautiful,
accepted,
loved;
flawed,
yes, in our flaky, makeshift 'normality' – but perfect
raw material
for the carpenter to make us newly,
truly,
divinely normal
according to his rule.

PROPER 20

Muckspreading

Amos 8:4-7

Muckspreading
(not to be confused with mud-slinging)
is an admirable activity, taken
both literally (provided the prevailing wind is in the right direction)
and particularly, in the words of Francis Bacon,
that 'money is like muck: good for nowt
unless 'tis well and truly spread about'.

What is money?
Money is wild pigs' teeth, treasure
to be traded for tobacco.
Money is a handful of change in my father's pocket, jingled,
irritatingly, when he was lost for words.
Money is a series of noughts on a piece of paper
(with or without a digit in front, in black or red).
Money is a high level virtual reality game, where the merest rumour
has repercussions that rock the real world and wreak havoc.

Money is
a driving force
a motivator
a confidence trick.
Money is power:
money talks

yes, money talks
but it is inclined to be economical with the truth.

Money is *not* muck,
neither is it the root of all evil,
as the super-spiritual (though unscriptural) among us might believe.

There is no particular merit
in treating whatever monies come our way
with cavalier indifference,
or a casual abandon that says we are above such things;
and don't let's be deceived:
pride can disguise itself as magnanimity or,
just as easily, embracing being poor.

Nor is it a privilege account
which buys our ultimate security
attracting, as it does, only fair weather friends,
purchasing a bright and brittle happiness
that lies, lies image-deep
commanding a kind of power, yes
but no authority: vulnerable, then
to the next highest bidder,
morality on the cheap,
the millionaire jumping to his own conclusion.

Yes, money talks
but it is inclined to be economical with the truth,

making extravagant claims for itself
whereas in reality
it is merely the debased coinage of *wealth*
every kind of wealth,
every kind of good thing which God has given to us
richly to enjoy
but also as a trust,
and a test
to see what we will make of it,
to see if we can resist the lure of the profit motive . . .

How did Amos know about Mars bars shrinking
and subsidies undermining Third World trade
and banks tempting students with overdrafts
and mortgage brokers offering loans of 100 per cent with no indemnity,
knowing they can always repossess the property;
and coffee barons robbing the growers' children of schooling and health

and multi-nationals pricing everyone else out of the market
and supermarkets caring more about the appearance of their fruit
than the welfare of their farmers;
and the world's richest countries oh so slowly relaxing their stranglehold
of debt repayments by the world's poor;
and economics, once the servant of philosophy and ethics
now the driving force of nations, the end in itself,
and almost any means justified
and – and –

Or perhaps he didn't know;
perhaps God gave us Amos, knowing human nature,
that what goes around, comes around
and the only thing we learn from history
is that we never learn from history,
precisely because human nature does not change,
just finds more up-to-the-moment ways of mucking things up.

But not, to return to Francis Bacon,
mucking things up in the right way – that is,
unloading the wealth we've received by the cartload,
spreading it with discernment, but also with gay abandon
in haste to make way for the next instalment
(for that's how it works, nature reflecting the ways of God)
spreading it, too, with *hilarity*
for God revels in giving, and calls us to share his joy.

And how do we know
where the next instalment may come from?

Already those countries to whom we once took the gospel
are sending their missionaries back to us;
how long, then, before we are the ones
in the pictures on the Christian Aid posters?

But this is not to corrupt our new-found generosity
with self-interest –
you were hungry and I fed you:
come on, you owe me one now!

Rather to note, with a certain wonder
and humbling of any incipient pride
that this, too, is the providence of God:
that we should learn never to depend
on wealth, whatever name it travels under –
dependence sits too close to worship;
rather we should learn, alongside
our giving, to be willing to receive
however, through whoever, whenever
God provides, trusting him
at the end of the day
to balance the scales.

Balance?
No, there's not much in Scripture about balance.
More about God saying, 'Go on, just try me!
Give as you should, and see if I will not open the windows of heaven
and drench you with blessing!'
'Give, and it will be given to you;
good measure, pressed down, shaken together, running over!
For the measure you give
will be the measure you get.'

To hell, then, with moderation:
let's give until it stops hurting,
give until we *must* depend on God, and
when the muck is well and truly spread
just see what grows . . .

PROPER 21

Hallelujah Tribute Band

Psalm 146

Praise the Lord.
That's an order,
all you guys! No more blues: go for the upbeat stuff;
not just you religious types (as if there were such a thing)
nor just when life is cool (cool is as you find it)
nor just in like-minded company (spread the word!)
Always, all ways, the bottom line is praise.

Praise the Lord, O my soul.
No hiding in the back row:
this one's got *my* name on it.
Lord, it's like you're on the mixing desk, hearing it all;
you know if I'm playing or miming; no one else
plays praise like me: without my riff, the track is incomplete
so, strut your thing, my soul!

I will praise the Lord all my life.
I will. Not just the rash, extravagant dream of young love
but a solemn declaration of intent;
I promise praise, whether in temptation, resignation,
adventure or retreat, gain or loss;
I'll praise the Lord that his love is for ever
and launches my life beyond death.

I will sing praise to my God as long as I live.
God, even if singing is not my thing (and you know it ain't!),
I'm setting my sights on knowing a joy in you
that words alone can never express
and somehow I'll find a way to show it:
let the dancer in me dance and the painter paint and the gardener grow
and the runner run rings round the earth for ever!

Do not put your trust in princes, mortal men.
'People always let you down,' my mother told me, and
'The more I see of people, the more I like dogs.'
Cynics apart, people are, after all, only human: man from dust,
earth to earth and a fair amount of dirt dished in between;
I can't blame my idols for letting me down – their own death means
they cannot help me through mine.

Blessed is he whose help is in the God of Jacob.
Praise the Lord for Jacob!
Go-getter, self-seeker, liar and fraud;
if God is willing to deal with him, even go down in history
as his Lord – there's hope for me and my mates yet.
And awesome to think I am part of the family tree
of those who belong to Jacob's God; I have a place in the scheme of things.

Maker of heaven and earth . . . who remains faithful for ever.
Praise is the only fit response
for you are behind and beyond it all, further than eye can see,
satellite probe or the mind of man conceive; you are the origin of
species,
you decided whether to start with a big bang
or the whisper of a word; you are the Mathematician,
Physician, Artist, Perfect Lover and Lord!

He upholds the cause of the oppressed.
Making poverty history
is hardly new; that's the depressing thing, it's there
in the law and the prophets, Jesus too; but the poor
are always here, imprisoned by drugs, or Aids, or debt,
famine or fear; I am humbled, Lord, that you are consistently on their
side
with your sleeves rolled up: am I?

The Lord lifts up those who are bowed down.
Lord, it must break your heart
to see so many bowed down in brokenness, weariness
bitterness, hopelessness. Can it be true that you lift them all,
now or later, inwardly if not outwardly – or do you wait to do it

through me? Lord, it must also break your heart
to see so few bowed down to worship and serve.

The Lord loves the righteous.
You know, Lord,
I've had a bit of an altercation with you over this:
OK, I realise that *righteous* is not *self-righteous* – you hate that
as much as I do – but you also said you loved *the world,*
every messy bit of it; perhaps, though, it is only those put right in Christ
you can love without qualification.

The Lord watches over the alien . . . the fatherless.
Lord, we honour your name!
Far from being to blame for the orphans and refugees
of the world, you are the number one aid agency,
bringing heaven to earth: earth, where stranger and child
are maligned and abused; heaven, where all have a father,
and all have come home.

He frustrates the way of the wicked.
To be honest, Lord, I don't see it:
but I have to take your word for it, because if you aren't straight
about one thing, then the whole package is suspect.
I can celebrate that light is greater than darkness,
love, in Christ, has overcome death: and sooner or later
evil must turn, or burn.

The Lord reigns for ever, your God, O Zion.
Reign? Rule? The whole authority thing
is a bit of a turn-off these days, but anarchy ruling
is not OK, and democracy drowns in a mire
of misunderstanding. Praise God, then, that he has a handle
on all this stuff. But why choose Zion, Lord?
Wasn't Birmingham good enough?

Praise the Lord!
Well, this is where I began
and where I will end
but never end.

PROPER 22

Waiting Room

Habakkuk 1:1-4, 2:1-4; Psalm 37:1-9

Hard benches
with chipped, shiny, dark-brown paint,
custard-yellow walls
and the wind whistling round my ankles:
can you wonder, Lord,
that when you tell me to *wait*
I am not enthusiastic?
I blame British Rail (as was) . . .

Unable to stop myself feeling sick
or concentrate on *Newsweek* magazine,
trying hard not to listen
but still hearing the drill shriek:
can you wonder, Lord,
that when you tell me to *wait*
I am not enthusiastic?
I blame the dentist . . .

Months and the phone doesn't ring
and then it's another man
who really wanted a garage
and open-plan living room:
can you wonder, Lord,
that when you tell me to *wait*
I am not enthusiastic?
I blame the estate agent . . .

The trouble with waiting
is that my expectations are low:
what, after all, can I hope for?
A late train, with standing room only;

a painful filling that one day will break again;
a reduction in price or a bridging loan;
waiting,
unfortunately, has a bad press
playing into the hands of the pessimist –
and, of late, the opportunist.
Why wait for the train?
Take the car, never mind the greenhouse gas;
Why go on the NHS waiting list?
Go private, never mind the ethical qualms;
Why risk losing the house of your dreams?
Take the loan, never mind the creeping debt;

Waiting,
a word waiting to be redeemed
for there are things that are worth waiting for:
ask the bridegroom,
the new mum and dad,
the heir apparent . . .
Though for all the joy,
the bride and groom will still have their bad hair days,
the parents their sleepless nights,
the heir his inheritance tax:

but the certain hope of heaven is all-embracing,
wholeness assured;
no ifs and buts
no small print
no qualification;
everything just right,
just and right
at last
and it will last
for ever.

Waiting,
room to grow
or time to kill?
If I think the promise is empty

I will become faithless, aimless;
if I think the promise too distant
I will become feckless, careless;

but the promise is true
and never, in God's economy, late
and time invested for God is guaranteed
eternal returns: nothing is wasted:
'Your battery charged, while you wait!'
and the fruits of the Spirit – while you wait.
'The statement of your account, while you wait!'
and the riches of Christ – while you wait.
'A dividend card, for you, while you wait!'
and the desires of your heart – while you wait
for the Lord in whom you delight
who will not disappoint or delay;

while you wait
on the Lord, in whom you delight,
who will not disappoint or delay.

For those who wait *on* the Lord
will renew their strength,
strength for today,
and hope for tomorrow.

Even this kind of waiting,
waiting *on* God
doesn't come easy;
the call for our undivided attention
in an age of instant messaging channel hopping web surfing
background music junk mail email
telemarketing instant loans and mobile phones – the call
to be still
and listen
and wait
is a bit counter-cultural
a bit retro
more than a bit of a challenge.

But it is the key,
it must be the key:
the room for waiting *on* God
so that he may fill our time between now and then
with trust, with anticipation,
with peace and with purpose
that leave no room for frustration
but are themselves the means of hastening the day
when Christ will rule with justice and mercy
and all corruption be rubbished away.

Wait
on God,
let him fill your mind's room,
and the minutes of each day;
his present
his presence
satisfying, and the time between *now*
and the promised future *then*
contentment:
not like waiting.

PROPER 23

You Won't Feel a Thing . . .

2 Kings 5:1-3, 6-15c; Luke 17:11-19

Coming from the dentist, it's a promise I long to hear
(though maybe a hollow one);
coming from almost anyone else
it's a threat
a threat and a warning
that something is seriously wrong.

You won't feel a thing . . .

Just imagine
popping that perfectly ripe grape into your mouth
and never feeling it burst against your teeth,
never feeling the sweetness of its juice on your tongue.
Just imagine
stroking velvet, or the soft skin of a baby's cheek
and never feeling that so gentle friction against your finger
that sends a tingle
up your arm and right to your heart.
Just imagine
adventuring step by step into the sea
and never feeling the ebb and flow as the water laps coolly, temptingly
over your feet and soaks your rolled up jeans.
Just imagine
hugging that frightened child, holding him tight
and never feeling the hot tears, the pressure of frantic fingers
around your neck beginning to ease.
Just imagine
receiving the kiss you dared not hope for
and never feeling it . . .

I imagine
it would destroy me,

destroy so much of what is most human in me;
destroy elation, anticipation,
pleasure: isolate me, destroy
my soul itself.

You won't feel a thing . . .

Just imagine
walking out in the biting winter night
and never feeling the sharp slap of the frost in your face,
the ache in your ears, the fumbling, stumbling of fingers and toes.
Just imagine
running your hand along splintery wood
and never feeling the punctured skin, the growing soreness
as flesh distends, and infection sets in.
Just imagine
sunbathing out on the beach
and never feeling the burning, blistering heat that stretches and bursts,
peeling layers of skin like microporous tape.
Just imagine
mowing the lawn that Monday morning
and never feeling the stabbing, constricting pain in your chest,
warning to stop, now! Your gardening days are numbered.
Just imagine
getting so close to the end of your tether
and never feeling the shock of banging your head on the wall
or tearing your hair, and so you go on, and on.

I imagine
it would destroy me.
Destroy my talent for self-protection,
destroy my instinct for survival,
my action, reaction; destroy
my body itself.

You won't feel a thing . . .

Just imagine
picking a daisy from your garden

and never feeling amazed by its complex simplicity:
wondering only how to get rid of them from your lawn.
Just imagine
phoning a friend in China
and never feeling awed by such a stupendous physical world:
wondering only at the engineer's brain and a slight delay on the line.
Just imagine
smashing an arm or leg
and never feeling knocked out by your body's power to heal itself:
wondering only at the weight of plaster, and the nurses' care.
Just imagine
watching the foetus grow in the womb
and never feeling humbled before this miracle of life:
wondering only how far we will one day design a child.
Just imagine
reading the arguments against God
and never feeling the divine nature of human reason:
wondering only why, though reason has the rhetoric, faith persists.

I imagine
it would destroy me,
destroy my capacity, my need
to wonder, even worship; to be still
and know that he is God; destroy
my Spirit itself.

You won't feel a thing:
like lepers
desensitised . . .

Here we are, then, ten lepers
desperate for sensation, but nine out of ten
sensitive only to what makes us, for the moment, feel good:
concerned only with body and soul,
with stimulation, relaxation,
absence of pain.

Nine lepers, who receive so much from the Lord
but only so much,

so much that is only skin-deep:
too easily satisfied,
we are not able
to be made whole

like the one leper, who received so much,
so much more, suddenly sensing
that health of body and soul
are bound up with wholeness of spirit;
who, returning, found himself
complete
at Jesus' feet . . .

The glory of God, they say,
is a person fully alive;
conversely, I can only be fully alive
when my sense of God is restored
and I give him the glory
for all the glory that shines in me.

Lord,
in this sensual age
when we have lost all sense
of you –
touch us,
heal us again.

PROPER 24

Flavour of the Month

Genesis 32:22-31; 2 Timothy 3:14 – 4:5; Luke 18:1-8

Raspberry ripple, or rum and raisin?
Alicante, or the South of France?
Blue or green for the garage door?
Learn to water ski, or ballroom dance?

You can spend a pleasurable few hours
flipping through brochures or *Which* magazine,
and if, at the end of the day, you find you hate the blue
why, you can always change it to green.

Shall I have my eyebrow pierced?
Perhaps I ought to take up Tae Kwon Do.
I wonder what it's like to snort cocaine
or skive off school and watch the flowers grow?

Well, give it a whirl, why not?
Send for the free samples,
test drive the 4 x 4
have the eight days' free trial;
this week, change your credit card company,
next week, your mortgage provider,
the week after that, your mobile phone,
your religion, or your partner –

why, you could make it an art form, a lifestyle:
there's always another flavour,
there's always a better deal.

Or that's what they'd have us believe.

I am so glad that God is not like that,
that he doesn't get bored
with making the sun rise every morning,

or think that there must be a better way to do it –
maybe try it today on a six-hour cycle, or from west to east?
And why should the tides be stuck with such a tedious table,
why not try four hours, or ten during school holidays?
Isn't gravity becoming overrated – why not
loosen it all up at the edges, and have
a little more levity?

Did God experiment, or did he always know
what was the best deal? Whatever . . .
How we need to trust, though
that he will opt, consistently, for the status quo.
For although God created 'butterfly'
he surely does not advocate
a flitting from friend to friend,
from partner to partner, from job to job,
from country to country, from god to god,
from one source of pleasure to the next;
flitting is for butterflies:
we, who are made in God's image, should surely model
commitment,
tenacity,
hanging on in there . . .

Like Jacob
who refused to let God go
any more than God would let him go,
wrestling his doubts during the long night,
knowing that the blessing of God,
not contrived or extorted but freely given
was the greatest good;

like the widow
who refused to let the judge sleep,
risking the neighbours' wrath
by her importunity,
knowing that, even when duty
and honour failed, perseverance could
see justice win through;

like Timothy
who refused to let the truth
be compromised to please a crowd
with itching ears, straining to hear the latest beat,
knowing that the word of God,
his truth alone, has power to
set the people free.

Three of a kind;
three with the grit
to commit to an exclusive passion;
three not afraid
to resist the temptation to flit
from attraction to attraction, for fear of missing
that definitive moment,
that defining experience
(like a teenager with a mobile phone
spending the evening ringing round, and round
and round again,
deciding on the coolest way
to spend the evening).

We are a strange race
where every other housewife seems to train
to join the thousands in the London marathon,
looking to be in it for the long haul,
to go the distance – great, but
we apply our dedication simply to a few miles
of metropolitan pavement
and an annual burst of charity.
Going the distance with marriage,
or principle,
or God
somehow doesn't seem to have the same appeal;
long-term marriage is boring and restrictive;
long-term employees are sad and unable to manage their own career;
long-term believers are bigoted and blinkered.

In an age of almost infinite possibility
it is somehow seen to be better to skim the oceans, go with the flow

than embark on a ship that is going somewhere
and not somewhere else;
in an age of almost infinite possibility
it is easy to give up too easily when 'it' doesn't seem to work for me
and move on, spending a lifetime comparing,
never pursuing.

But God
rewards faith,
without which it is impossible to please him,
faith that says *I will not let you go.*
Though at times you don't appear to hear me, and I could say
this thing does not seem to work for me
I won't give up, precisely for the reason that I know
you do hear and will reward me according to
the seriousness of my searching . . .

Butterflies, I think, were created
to be appreciated,
not imitated
as icons of consumer choice:

let's rock the boat
and vote
commitment
flavour of the month . . .

PROPER 25

Crocodile Tears

Jeremiah 14:7-10, 19-22; Psalm 84:1-7

Was it a natural disaster,
or an act of God?
From the Press, it would seem
that Christians are saying the former: Muslims the latter.
But if the God of the Old Covenant commanded war and famine,
drought and pestilence and plague –
what of the God of the New?
Did he suddenly cease to be as instrumental
in the orchestration of his world?
Surely he is the same God, the great composer who,
unlike Beethoven, is not deaf to the implications of his works
(including the spanners thrown in by the foolishness of men
and the fiendishness of devils)
but weaves all manner of things together
in the build-up to the grand finale?

If there is purpose, then,
as well as consequence
in such catastrophes
let us not only ask 'How can God allow such a thing to happen?'
but expect an answer:
and expect to be changed by the answer.

That's what they said in Judah,
in Jeremiah's day, in the midst of the drought –
'How can God allow such a thing to happen?
Where is he? Why does he seem to us
like a tourist, noting the sights and passing on?
Like a travelling salesman, finding few openings for business and passing on?

Like a workman shaking his head at the job,
saying "No, sorry, can't help you there . . ." and passing on?'

It even crossed their minds that they might, somehow, be to blame:
'Lord, we have sinned against you,
and so did our fathers
but do something, Lord, for the sake of your name!'
And God does hear – but he hears
only words, empty words
and crocodile tears.

He hears only the word from a hungry belly
and listens in vain for the cry of a hungry heart;
he hears only the word from a thirsty tongue
and listens in vain for the gasp of a thirsty soul;
he hears only the word from those who were once wealthy
and listens in vain for the will to be rich in spirit;
he hears only the word from the landowner losing his living
and listens in vain for the longing for *life.*

God hears, but he hears only sorrow, and not repentance;
only words, empty words
and crocodile tears.

Their soul does not yearn for the presence of God,
their heart and their flesh do not cry out for him;
they've made no commitment to walk with the Lord;
they just want
the rain to come – or go
the fever to pass
the debt to be cleared
the fighting to stop
the sun to come out
and everything in the garden to be lovely once more:

but they don't want God,

they don't want God to do it *his* way,
they don't want to hear

that when they pass (as they must) through the Valley of Tears
it is only real tears
that will feed those living springs:
not crocodile tears.

The Valley of Tears –
valley formed by glaciers of isolation,
poverty, exploitation or despair;
valley formed by the quarrying out of suffering
throwing up slag-heaps of resignation, where
weeds grow up and create a deceptive greening;
fine veneer
screening the emptiness.

When we pass (as we must) through the Valley of Tears
what is it to us?
An emptiness to be filled with shallow regret,
with petulant protests, anger or listlessness?
Or an emptiness, perhaps to be disguised
by making the best of a bad job,
putting a brave face on our wistfulness
or our anguish as hope dies?

Or is it an emptiness to be probed by the searchlight of God
dispelling the myth of our self-sufficiency;
an emptiness demanding to be confessed,
that lack of patient endurance and real love;

an emptiness which in fact is a gift from above
to provoke, and receive our tears,
tears wrung from the depths of our being
becoming for us springs of the grace of God?

As we walk (as we must) through the Valley of Tears,
through the places of hardship,
there it is we become
deeper, fuller;
as we fight the good fight and finish the race,
refuse to give up or give in,

there it is we become
humbler, stronger;
as we see the true state of ourselves and our world,
see as God sees,
there it is we become
homesick for heaven.

Cry to God!
Let your heart cry, and you will find him
in quake and in quiet;
cry for God!
Let your heart be open for him to fill it,
stir it, guide it;
cry for real,
for though he hears, sadly he turns away
from our crocodile tears.

London Road

Ephesians 1:11-23; Luke 6:20-31

How many towns in England have a London Road?
Hundreds, I dare say:
most of those within a hundred miles of London
and it's not a misnomer, or a deception:
of course those roads are not *in* London,
and those who travel on them have not yet arrived in London
yet, in a sense their destination is fixed
because they have committed themselves to that road
and one day they will enjoy the full experience
of all that London can offer . . .

Neither is it a misnomer, or a deception
for you to call me, or me to call you 'saint':
certainly we have not yet arrived
yet our destination is fixed
because we have committed ourselves to the Lord
and one day we will enjoy the full experience
of all that he can offer . . .

Was it right for me to be dissatisfied
with what my little town or village could offer?
Was it right to leave –
perhaps to leave family, friends –
and set out on a long, sometimes a hard road?
And what did I really know about London?
Would it be all it was cracked up to be?
There were some who even said,
how did I know there *was* such a place –
never actually seen it, had I?

But yes: I believe I was right
not to be satisfied with being poor,

with the poverty of spirit I sensed in my little town,
and in myself. I knew I could be more,
should be more – should be lighter, deeper,
giving more of myself
having more of myself to give; I could not ignore
that sense of calling to greater heights and depths
that filled me with apprehension, yet
compelled me to take to the road,
and seek my fortune.

Yes, I believe I was right
to see that my hunger would not be met
by club or pub, improving health, wealth, or
a change of house or spouse.
This was a hunger for peace and integration,
for putting together the pieces of my life
in a way that made some sort of sense;
and I think that I caught, on the lid of the box
a glimpse of my destination,
and in my ear, a whisper:
'Turn again! Worthy citizen not of this place
but of London Town . . .'

Yes, I believe I was right
to see that my tears were more
than tears of self-pity: tears, rather, for a world
wasting its God-given wealth,
wasting away; for a people too easily pleased
with themselves, who perceive
neither your pain nor your promise;
tears, too, that I belong to this world, this people
but I wish it were not so:
I wish I was on a different road . . .

Yes, I believe I was right
to choose that different road, in spite of the taunts
of trying to be holier than thou,
in spite of the indignation that, somehow,
I was criticising their lifestyle, their town;

in spite of the so-called superior wisdom
which said I was on a hide into nothing,
a road to nowhere; a sign saying 'London'
couldn't be more than a piece of graffiti,
some kind of inferior cosmic joke.

It is right not to settle
not to settle for anything less
than all we are called to be:
holy,
for I am holy, says your Lord and God.

It is right to take note
of these stirrings of the Spirit
of these intimations of greatness
of these hints of heaven
of this call to be saints:
of this holy smoke,
sure sign of holy fire.

It is right
to trust,
to trust ourselves to the road,
to trust ourselves
to the one who calls such travellers 'saints':
to the one whose holy fire
will unmake us,
remake us –
then, no longer saints in the making
but saints through and through,
citizens of a world
ordered to run on holiness;
a world to be called
heaven

which may
or may not
bear more than a passing resemblance
to London . . .

FOURTH SUNDAY BEFORE ADVENT

You Make Me Sick

Isaiah 1:10-18; Psalm 32:1-7; Luke 19:1-10

'Hear the word of the Lord, you rulers of Sodom;
listen to the law of our God, you people of Gomorrah!'
And that was the leaders and the people of Israel –
I bet that shook them.
Or, if you like, the bishops and churchgoing folk of today –
Ouch.

'The multitude of your services – what are they to me?' says the Lord.
'I have had more than enough of altar candles,
of sanctuary lamps and votive tea-lights;
I have no pleasure
in beautifully embroidered hassocks and banners.
When you come to appear before me,
who has asked this of you,
this prettification of my house?
Stop bringing meaningless offerings!
Your perfunctory praying is detestable to me.
Your Saints days, Sundays and synods –
I cannot bear your evil assemblies.
Your Saints days and your special services
my soul hates.
They have become a burden to me;
I am weary of bearing them . . .'

What, Lord? You can't mean us – you can't mean *my* church!
But perhaps he can. And perhaps he'll decide (like a lot of other people)
not to go to church any more;
perhaps there are even churches where he hasn't been for ages,
but no one noticed.

'When you spread out your hands in prayer
I will not listen;

your hands are full of photocopied empty words
and blood, my life's blood, which you have allowed to seep unchecked
from your cutting apart of my Word.
Stop pretending! Start mending your ways: seek justice!
Then, when you pray, expect that salvation will come.'

Lord, we see that our sin makes you sick;
we would fear for our lives
had you not said that although our sins are like scarlet
they will be white as snow:
in the place of well-deserved judgement, grace intervenes.

'Blessed is the one who has been forgiven
for doing wrong
and for failing to do what is right;
the one who has ceased to kid himself
that his trifling misdemeanours and oversights
don't really matter;
the one who knows that, whilst the Lord is gracious,
he is not to be trifled with . . .

When I buried my head in the sand
my very body protested;
all kinds of aches and pains beset me,
for day and night
you were nudging me, trying to get my attention;
I was stressed, heading for burnout,
on the verge of a breakdown . . .'

What, you mean that all these problems with my health
are really to do with my spiritual health?
That if I deal with my denial,
denial of anger and disappointment,
bitterness, idleness, lack of love –
that I will be healed?
Well, when doctors say that so many problems they're asked to treat
have no physical cause or cure
it has to be worth a trial.

'I said, "I will confess to the Lord
and call my sin by its name" –
and you forgave
the guilt which betrayed itself in every part of my being,
and made me whole.
You are my great physician
and the sanctuary of my soul;
when the outside world does its worst
my inside world is forearmed, at one with you.'

Lord, we see that our sin makes us sick;
we would fear for our lives
were it not that you said to the paralysed man
'Your sins are forgiven: take up your bed, and walk!'
In the place of well-deserved judgement, grace intervenes.

And now, meet Zacchaeus, taxman,
Jericho's leading capitalist
living a life of luxury,
posh house in the fashionable part of town,
abusing his ancestry by collaborating with Roman rule,
abusing his position by ripping off the man in the street,
abusing his own integrity by practising fraud and deceit.

Do we recognise him?
The latest politician to be pilloried by the press,
the latest businessman to be tried for insider dealing,
the latest civil servant to provide a lucrative leaked document . . .
Small men
lacking the stature to say no to temptation;
in the eyes of the people,
the lowest of the low.

But Jesus saw through the leaves of the tree,
knew his desire to climb free from the tangle of guilt,
and embraced the public sinner:
hearing the reservations of those who were sinned against,
asked them to marvel at the growth of a new man

whose change of heart restored his soul
and their fortunes . . .

Lord, we see that our sin makes others sick;
we would fear for our lives
were it not that you said that although it is hard for a rich man
to enter the kingdom of heaven, with God all things can be possible.
In the place of well-deserved judgement, grace intervenes.

Sin,
the single cause
making you sick
making me sick
making others sick

and the double cure
repentance and grace.

THIRD SUNDAY BEFORE ADVENT

Aunt Sally

Job 19:23-27a; Luke 20:27-38

Popular lady, Aunt Sally;
enjoying quite a resurrection today
(despite the demise of the old-fashioned fairground).

Set 'em up
knock 'em down, set 'em up
knock 'em down –
the cardboard cut-outs
that pass for reasons not to believe;
hurl your ridicule
and down they go, not a leg to stand on.
But it's only a game,
isn't it?

The classic, of course, is the long white beard
and the old man who is everyone's grandfather.
Blake and Michelangelo, I fear
you have a lot to answer for:
the Ancient of Days and the ceiling of the Sistine chapel
may be masterpieces
of misleading;
who one earth, they say, can believe in such a God?
Who indeed?
No Christian I know.

That's no God; that's an Aunt Sally.

Then, of course, there's the devil with horns,
pitchfork and evil little goblin face, courtesy of
Hieronymus Bosch
and echoed in every fantasy computer game; worn

caricature, contriving to conceal
the real evil that all the rain of heaven
will not wash from our world:
who on earth, they say, can believe in such a devil?
Who indeed?
No Christian I know.

That's no devil; that's an Aunt Sally.

And what's all this about life after death?
Surely the Sadducees had it right: make hay
while the sun shines, there's no second bite at the cherry.
Sitting around all day
strumming harps, like some spaced-out, celestial boy band
stuck in the groove for ever and ever?
No way!
Who on earth, they say, can believe in a life after death like that?
Who indeed?
No Christian I know.

That's no resurrection being; that's an Aunt Sally.

So let's join in the sport,
shake hands with the cynics and
laugh these Aunt Sallies once and for all out of court,
knocking 'em down so flat
they can never bounce back.
And now
redraw the lines of battle,

now that we can see,
behind those cardboard cut-outs,
what Christians *really* believe.

Now there's a challenge
and I don't mean just for the cynics.

Gone the white-whiskered patriarch: fine!
But what takes his place?

In the face of abuse and divorce and sperm donation
we must somehow recover Fatherhood;
in the face of sweeping assumptions of evolution
we must somehow recover creation;
with those who prefer to travel hopefully than to arrive
we must speak of authority, and of revelation.

Gone the grimacing gremlin in red and black: fine!
But what takes his place?
In the face of the frequent and widespread temptation
to locate evil somewhere – anywhere – outside of ourselves;
in the face of the media's demonisation
of this month's rapidly moving target
we must have the courage to name both the evil within
and the evil that claims for itself the role of God.

Gone are the all-night gigs in cloud city: fine!
But what takes their place?
In the face of an ever-aging population
encouraged to cling to every last lingering flicker of life,
in the face of renewed ideas of reincarnation
and accusations of pie in the sky
we must dare to announce the hope of a lively heaven
where God wipes the tears from every eye
and all is made whole . . .

Can we do it?
Can we take our brash and brittle world by the hand,
take them beyond the Aunt Sallies
to where Jesus stands
on the street corner with the manky dog,
leaning on the bar at the comedy club,
queuing for the high street sales –
and know how to introduce them to each other?
To where he sits
at the next desk but one in the office,
at the check-out in the superstore,
glued to the internet in the small hours –
whatever will they make of one another?

Can I tell them?
Can I tell them what it means to me, that God *is*
and is the God of Jesus Christ?
Really, what difference does it make
that I have a father in heaven
and how do I picture a God who is personal, yes, but Spirit?

Can I tell them?
Can I tell them what it means to me, that the devil *is*
and is a proud, fallen angel, liar and thief?
Really, what difference does it make
that I have an enemy at my heels
and how do I picture evil which is personal, yes, but Spirit?

Can I tell them?
Can I tell them what it means to me, that there *is* life after death
and it's what we were made for?
Really, what difference does it make
that I have my sights set beyond the grave
and how do I picture a heaven which is too real for my earthly senses?

You can see why Aunt Sally
manages, somehow, to hang on in there: why we still
find Don Quixote tilting at so many windmills.
But it's no good; we must lay their ghosts in our own lives,
lay them to rest
and do our best
to give the cynics some real-life targets,
trusting our Father in heaven to deliver us from evil,
and show them his kingdom, his power and his glory.

SECOND SUNDAY BEFORE ADVENT

Idle Thoughts

2 Thessalonians 3:6-13

IDLE is just another way of spelling LIED

and we all know who is the father of lies.

He lied to the Thessalonian church
when he told them that Jesus was coming soon
so they could just sit back,
take it easy, and wait to be whisked away
any minute now,
to live happily ever after.

He lies to our churches today
when he tells us that Jesus is *not* coming soon
so we can just sit back,
take it easy, and wait to be whisked away
eventually
to live happily ever after.

REST is a recommendation of God;
IDLENESS is an aberration,
temptation. *Satan finds some mischief still*
for idle hands to do . . .

While there is bread to be broken,
lessons prepared,
truths to be spoken
and joys to be shared;
tears to be shouldered
and fields to be farmed,
kids to be cared for
and fears to be calmed,

can love remain idle?

While there are families floundering,
children abused
peace efforts foundering
refuge refused;
millions malnourished
while we overeat
and millions more dying
of ills we could treat,

can love remain idle?

Love has an aim and an object and,
if it is not expressed in word and deed
I may doubt it is real.
Idling is failing to love,
squandering energy,
engine running, going nowhere . . .

But did the idle deserve *such* a pounding
from Paul, a dressing-down
worthy of a drill sergeant
bawling out the parade ground?
It's only *idleness*, after all –
a sin of omission,
not like murder.
But remember the mischief?

The idle curiosity
that makes me into
a busybody, a voyeur
a critic and a creep?

The idle gossip
that topples a man,
kicks him while he's down,
stabs him in the back?

The idle thought
never brought captive to Christ

that opens the door
to deflection, deception?

The idle
are a burden to the church
which has more pressing, more
eternally important things to do.

The idle
are their own worst enemy,
abusing the means of grace,
refusing the means of growth.

The idle
are a disgrace to God,
depressing his image,
suppressing his Spirit.

Now, as then,
a present-day Paul would make short shrift
of pew-warmers, TV Christians,
those whose faith is little more
than a spectator sport;
those who through ignorance, apathy or fear
refuse to get stuck in,
dirty their hands, tax their brains,
ring out laughter, wring out tears,
take their faith out into the ring
and win a few rounds . . .

If we want to see our churches grow,
it's not a case of getting bums on seats
but off them.

When Christ comes –
and that is not in doubt,
only if it be sooner
or later – when he comes
he will be the judge

of whether our faith, and our hope, and our love
are real; whether in fact
they have stirred us to action

or whether our faith has been a fair-weather faith,
our hope more like wishful thinking,
our so-called love
idle.

My salvation, my home in heaven,
these are secure: both depend
not on my work
but on my acceptance
of God's grace.
But what a disgrace
and a cause of overwhelming regret
if my life's work disappears in the fire
of wood, hay and stubble,
faulty goods, damaged beyond repair
by the deadly sin of sloth.

When Christ returns,
will he find faith on earth?
Will he find his body in good working order,
ears listening, eyes scanning,
hands building, feet running,
voice praising, heart beating

with the love that cannot remain idle?

CHRIST THE KING

Jesus: The Interview

Colossians 1:11-20; Luke 23:33-43

I (to himself) I have a feeling that this one may not go quite as planned; he has a bit of a reputation for turning the tables. Oh well, here goes! Jesus, you've been called many things in your time: how would you describe yourself?

J That rather depends on the company I'm in.

I A true politician's answer!

J Now that's something I've *never* been called – troublemaker, yes; the truth, yes; bringer of peace, yes, but not at any price. Good Shepherd is a bit of a personal favourite: so many people are well-meaning but woolly-headed – and lost.

I When you were a child, what did you want to be when you grew up?

J I always wanted to follow in my father's footsteps: taking the material God provides and cutting it, forming it, shaping it into something useful and beautiful.

I Tables, yokes for ploughing, lintels –

J No, people, mainly: though the carpentry was a good preparation.

I What do you drive?

J Drive? Where do you get these questions from? Well, I drive some to distraction – my mother, mainly, and doctors of law; and hypocrites to high fury. And some, I hope, into the arms of God: sheep into the sheepfold.

I I was thinking of transport, actually.

J Oh, sorry! Shanks's pony, mainly; boats; donkeys for special occasions. Is that relevant?

I It's a new angle – a king on a donkey?

J New? To you, maybe; in the kingdom of heaven, value judgements are void, because everyone is valued infinitely. Royalty is redefined. Donkeys are the new Daimlers.

I And *are* you King of the Jews? I'm not sure you ever made that clear.

J All who accept the rule of a king belong to his kingdom; in the kingdom of heaven there are no boxes marked 'ethnic origin' to tick.

I And your favourite holiday destination . . .

J Holiday? Do you mean holy day? Taking time to focus on God . . . hills are good, or the lake at sunrise.

I Of course, I guess you never travelled far; tourism wasn't invented!

J There's an amazing valley, though, up in the Atlas mountains; and the Great Barrier Reef –

I What? How do you know?

J I did have a bit of a say in the design. It was such fun, you know, drawing up that master plan, seeing our words become worlds, seeing what God-ness looked like, felt like, how everything hung together, worked together, just like we did . . .

I We?

J Doesn't anyone go to church these days? 'In the name of the Father, and of the Son, and of the Holy Spirit.'

I Ah, church – that's another thing. What do you think of the church today?

J Don't get me started.

I But aren't you its head?

J So they say. But they will treat 'church' as an institution and me as its general manager: God help us! Institutionalise God, and you get religion: and religion is a kill . . . I should know. Church isn't always what it seems; church is everyone who truly accepts me as 'head' – and we can be a pretty unorthodox, ragbag army; not necessarily welcome on a Sunday morning; not susceptible to rules and regulations, surveys or statistics – but I tell you, we're going places: we are the future!

I Ye–es. So the church isn't on its way out?

J Over my dead body! The fact that you have a gothic-looking art gallery down the road has very little to do with it. Think global! Think backwards and forwards in time! One day, everything and everyone will be gathered in, and will realise that *God is God*; I will stand at the watershed and they will all look me in the eye and then pass on, to right or left.

I Er . . . if I can bring you back to the present – what do you like to do in your spare time?

J I don't understand what you mean by spare time. Every minute is given by God for a purpose, whether it's teaching or learning, fishing or eating, building up or pulling down, reaping, sleeping or putting the rubbish out. Like? Well, I do like a good party – I am human, you know!

I And also, some would say, divine?

J You have the evidence.

I I do?

J If you care to look. After all, I've been on trial now for a couple of thousand years. You've had critical scholars examining all the documents, psychologists debating my sanity, scientists dissecting my miracles, cowards debunking my claims; sift through all that if you will – or else, go back to the Bible and tell me, who is this Jesus you find there . . . What do you think?

I Think? I think – the jury's still out; I will say, though, that some of your answers – and questions – leave me feeling uneasy; disorientated. I am not sure that our roles aren't becoming reversed; I'm not quite sure how to end this interview: forgive me.

J That is a very good ending.